P9-DBZ-067

"In light of recent events, these points of view are now even more relevant to gaining a perspective on the nation's union activities."
—*Newsday*

HOFFA
The Real Story
by James R. Hoffa
as told to Oscar Fraley

STEIN AND DAY/Publishers/New York

Distributed by Whirlwind Book Company

First STEIN AND DAY PAPERBACK edition, 1976

First published in 1975
Copyright © 1975 by James R. Hoffa and Oscar Fraley
Library of Congress Catalog Card No. 75-28207
All rights reserved
Designed by David Miller
Printed in the United States of America
Stein and Day/*Publishers*/Scarborough House
Briarcliff Manor, N.Y. 10510
ISBN 0-8128-2099-1

To my wife Jo,

the love of my life

and

To

THE NATIONAL ASSOCIATION FOR JUSTICE

FOR ITS MAGNIFICENT

WORK IN PENAL REFORM

Contents

1. I'll Be Back   9

2. How It All Started   21

3. Jo   39

4. The Rise to Power   49

5. The Spoiled Brat   61

6. The Start of the Frame-up   75

7. Gangsters and the "Irish Mafia"   87

8. The Board of Monitors   101

9. Two Killings Averted   109

10. Chattanooga Choo-choo   117

11. You Can't Beat City Hall   129

12. Convict   137

13. Outside Again   155

14. The National Association for Justice   167

     Bumper Sticker   177

     AN EPILOGUE BY OSCAR FRALEY

1

I'll Be Back

I made two disastrous mistakes in my life.

The first was coming to grips with Robert F. Kennedy to the point where we became involved in what can only be called a blood feud. The result was that I became John F. Kennedy's steppingstone to the White House. And then the brothers Kennedy railroaded me to prison in March of 1967 and I spent four years and ten months in Lewisburg Penitentiary.

My second mistake was naming Frank Fitzsimmons as my successor. Maybe I should say my steward. Because everyone knew that I intended to come back and take over again as president of the International Brotherhood of Teamsters, Chauffeurs, Warehousemen and Helpers of America.

In the ten years I was president of the Teamsters, I had raised the membership from eight hundred thousand to more than 2 million and made it the largest single labor union in the world. As I faced going to prison I spent a lot of hours worrying about who to endorse to carry on while I was away.

The choice came down to either Harold Gibbons, who for a long time had been one of my most loyal supporters, or Frank Fitzsimmons, a guy I took off a 3-C Highway Company truck and hand-carried all the way from shop steward to general vice-president.

I booted it. I picked Fitzsimmons.

For as it turned out, Fitzsimmons coveted the general presidency on a permanent basis. He forgot who made him when he got Washingtonitis.

He knew damned well that when I stood for reelection, he didn't have the chance of an ice cube in hell. So he was the man who had conditions attached to my commutation when I was released from prison in December of 1971—conditions which were unconstitutional and which I knew nothing about when I signed the mandatory release papers—which were designed to keep me from any union activities until 1980.

Don't take my word for it. Consider this report from the August, 1974, *Reader's Digest*, written by Lester Velie, a "roving editor":

> Fitzsimmons found himself in the classic posture of the man to whom a best friend has entrusted a best girl.
>
> He fell in love with the girl—the Teamster presidency—and moved aggressively to keep her.
>
> For Fitzsimmons, a phlegmatic, pumpkin-faced 66-year-old with a heavy belly, the girl had many attractions. First there was the handsome dowry, a $125,000 yearly salary. Then there were three homes to live in—one in California, one in Florida and another in Washington—and a $3.5 million jet plane that would carry him anywhere in the world, all expenses paid. To this, finally, was added the courtship of the President of the United States. Seeking labor support, President Nixon met with Fitzsimmons' executive board in the summer of 1971, rubbed elbows with mob-connected officials, and let it be known that the White House door was always open to Fitzsimmons.

That's Frank Fitzsimmons, a man who would have done almost anything to keep the Teamsters' presidency. And he did.

I charge Fitzsimmons with political influence peddling and conspiring with John Dean and Charles Colson of President Richard Nixon's "Watergate staff" to prevent me from regaining my office.

I charge him with selling out to mobsters and letting known racketeers into the Teamsters.

I charge him with blackjacking union officials into line by giving $7 million in annual organizing funds only to people who promise to support him.

I charge him with sending Hoffa supporters among the Teamster officials to "Siberia" so they couldn't influence delegates to the 1976 convention.

I charge him with awarding a $1.3 million Teamster "public-relations" program in 1973 to two men with criminal records.

I charge him with permitting underworld establishment of a union insurance scheme which in one year was a ripoff to the tune of $1,185,000 in the New York area alone and in which his own son, Don, participated on a national level.

I charge him with making vast loans from the billion-dollar Teamster pension fund to known mobsters.

I charge him with winning Teamster support by giving regional union officials powers that belong to the International executive board.

I charge him with stripping my wife and my son of union posts as a further means of undermining my influence.

There will be more and more developments as time goes on and I get my hands on additional information. For when the conditions on my commutation are lifted—as I am certain they will be—I *will* be back as president of the Teamsters.

There have been reliable reports that ever since Fitzsimmons took over the underworld holds the balance of power in the Teamsters. I have heard on good authority that without "the boys" Fitzsimmons couldn't remain in office as president.

Well, mobsters be damned! There is evidence that no less than 83 percent of the membership is behind me and when I am back you can be damned sure that heads will roll.

Fitzsimmons has tried like hell to keep me out of the way and his big move was in conspiring to have conditions placed on my commutation that would prevent me knocking him out of the box in the 1976 Teamster presidential election. I'd gone to prison on March 7, 1967, in a frame-up that I'll detail later on. On March 3, 1971, the U.S. Parole Board denied my petition for parole. The reason, I know for sure, was because at that time Fitzsimmons hadn't completed his deal to hang me by the thumbs.

On June 22, 1971, I resigned my last remaining Teamster position on the advice that it was blocking my parole. That was as president of my original Local 299 in Detroit—and Fitzsimmons' son, Richard, immediately moved up in that local.

Six more months went by before I was notified I would be commuted. It had given Fitzsimmons time to make his deal with Colson, who went up the river himself later in the Watergate mess, and with Dean, who ratted on President Nixon to take the lid off the Watergate cesspool.

Fitzsimmons, Dean, and Colson conspired to have conditions attached to my commutation which would keep me out of union activities until 1980. Colson's payoff was that his new law firm would receive the bulk of Teamster legal business at a pretty fat fee of one hundred thousand dollars a year plus. Dean's interest was that Fitzsimmons agreed to back Nixon in his 1972 campaign for reelection.

Dean suggested the conditions to John Mitchell, then the attorney general, and I have an affidavit from Mitchell that he told Dean that he questioned the legality of the conditions. But more on that later. The fact is that after that they simply bypassed Mitchell.

When my sentence was commuted finally in December, 1971, there were no conditions against union activity on the form I signed.

It knocked me flat when I learned the next day from a reporter at the airport that there was another commutation document signed by Nixon—which I hadn't seen and hadn't even been told about—barring me from union activity until four years after the 1976 Teamster presidential election.

If I'd known of those conditions I never would have accepted the commutation. Hell, I'd have been free without any restrictions in 1974.

Colson supposedly got religion when he went to the can. But he still proved himself a no-good liar. I mean he's both no good and no good at lying, because he said that George Meany and Leonard Woodcock both had urged Nixon to keep me out of union work. Both Meany and Woodcock denied it.

Meanwhile, Fitzsimmons was using all his clout in Washington to make himself seem lily-white. *Overdrive* is a magazine which reaches just about everybody in the trucking business. The magazine had given me some lumps in the past. Now it jumped on Fitzsimmons with an article in which it spelled out his dealings with Washington officials in return for special favors. Congressman Sam Steiger of Arizona was supposed to have the article put in the *Congressional Record*.

Fitzsimmons purportedly asked former Attorney General Richard G. Kleindienst to have it kept out. Whatever, it didn't get in.

All the while Fitzsimmons was using the power and patronage of the union presidency to blackjack union officials into line, particularly those known as Hoffa supporters, and to line up mobster support against the day he knew I'd be running at him.

He gave regional Teamster officials powers that didn't belong to them—powers that should be held by the international executive board. On top of this, the Teamsters set aside $7 million a year for organizing purposes. He awarded this jackpot only to Fitzsimmons supporters and began sending my people to the boondocks.

A case in point was Charles (Chuckie) O'Brien, more of a son of mine than a protégé since he was six years old. I made O'Brien an international organizer and he was told by Fitzsimmons that he was going to be sent to Alaska. Word filtered down to me that O'Brien "made peace" with Fitzsimmons and was to get, instead of the freeze-out, a plush assignment to Florida. Proving, I guess, that self-preservation really is the first law of nature no matter what they say about biting the hand that feeds you.

Hitting as close to home as possible, Fitzsimmons also had my wife, Jo, fired as head of DRIVE, the union's political arm, and he eliminated my son, Jimmy, as a Teamster lawyer. Both of their appointments had been approved by the membership. Fitzsimmons just arbitrarily eliminated them.

But now let's get down to the nitty-gritty. What I mean by that is the way Teamster business patronage lately has been turning up in hoodlum hands.

Fitzsimmons last year approved a $1.3 million "public-relations program" for the Teamsters. Part of the money went to a pair of "image improvers" with criminal records. One of them had actually served twenty years on a murder rap.

Then there was the severance-fringe benefit scheme he approved for underworld figure Louis Ostrer and from which Fitzsimmons' son, Don, benefited. It milked more than $1,185,-000 out of the pockets of Teamster members in the New York–New Jersey area alone.

Ostrer pleaded guilty in 1969 to swindling a Canadian insurance company out of $338,000. He received a five-year suspended sentence. While he was on probation he was convicted on a federal stock swindling charge in company with "Johnny Dio" Dioguardi. Both of them were linked to the New York Mafia and a New York County indictment also charged Ostrer was connected with Mafia loan sharks. It was alleged that he had discussed the proposed slaying of a borrower who was delinquent.

Ostrer came up with a union insurance scheme and sold it to Teamster Local 295 in New York, which had become dominated by labor racketeer Harry Davidoff. Under the plan, trucking employers paid forty dollars a week for each employee to buy individual insurance policies for union members and build a severance-pay fund. The employers were told to buy, or else.

Then—and the charges were brought by the New York State Insurance Department—the employers' payments were siphoned off by outrageous commissions and administration fees. State investigators charged that the insurance which cost the fund $1,238,274 should have cost only $52,546. The skim was better than $1,185,000.

Consider that the employers were paying the money instead of giving wage increases, which means that it was coming out of the employees' pockets.

This swindle was so successful in New York and New Jersey that Ostrer figured, what the hell, let's give the whole country a shot. But now he needed the support of Frank Fitzsimmons, who was making big waves as general president of the Teamsters and riding high with the Nixon bunch. If you have the president of the United States in your pocket there aren't going to be too many investigative agencies crawling up your back.

Ostrer has been quoted as saying he needed a "conduit" in order to meet "certain people." Namely Frank Fitzsimmons. So he went to Detroit in 1972 and hired Fitzsimmons' son, Don, as a so-called consultant and publicity man. Of course it didn't matter that Don Fitzsimmons had no insurance experience and was peddling vending machines for a hoodlum-owned company.

Besides, as Don Fitzsimmons admitted, he was looking for "something lucrative." Which this scheme certainly was.

Ostrer said that Frank Fitzsimmons "quickly saw the value of my plan and told me I could go out and sell it to Teamster locals on its merits." With the approval of the general president, which is a tremendous amount of clout in a scheme like this one, the "merits" were quick to be seen and the profits were gigantic.

Don Fitzsimmons, who said he was looking for something big at that time, lined up unions in Michigan, California, Nevada, New Jersey, Massachusetts, and Illinois. It has been estimated that more than sixty, and maybe more than seventy, Teamster locals in those states and in Florida were saddled with the plan.

God only knows how much was clipped out of that operation.

The Teamsters' Central States, Southeast and Southwest Area Pension Fund has become the biggest mob target of them all. Employers of a half million Teamsters contribute more than $200 million to this pension fund every year. This has created a fund of more than $1 billion. You don't just let that money sit there. It is loaned out at the going rate of interest.

During my years as general president I made loans to what the government labeled suspicious characters, if not charging them with being outright mobsters. I'll go into that later. But I'll tell you one thing for damned sure. We had damned few defaults.

Which is more than can be said now. The mob has pulled some pretty slick operations. They get a guy to front for them and obtain a huge loan. Who the hell knows what happens to the money, whether somebody went out and bought a yacht or stuck it into their pocket? All of a sudden the company goes broke, bankruptcy is filed, and the union sits there holding an empty bag. The mob can walk in to a legitimate businessman who needs cash. They have the contacts to get the loan and he fronts it. But he better not push them for too much of the money or he just might be rubbed out.

In this connection, Harvey Leach, chairman of the board of the Joshua Doore Furniture Company in Detroit, revealed his connection with the mob to federal investigators. He was "hit" on March 16, 1974. His throat was cut from ear to ear.

Somebody tried to put a hit recently on Allen Dorfman, who arranged a lot of loans for interests in Chicago. It was pretty well known that mobsters in the East were red-assed because they weren't getting what they considered was their fair share of the pension-fund action.

One of those who came to the joint when I was in Lewisburg was Anthony (Tony Pro) Provenzano. He had been head of Teamster Local 560 in Hoboken, New Jersey. Tony had been nailed on an extortion rap. As far as I was concerned, that ruled him out from then on as a union official. He asked me to use my influence to let him keep his Teamster pension. I said no dice. End of "friendship."

Well, since he has been out, Provenzano has been involved in Florida building projects which involve more than $5 million in Teamster pension fund loans.

When I was railroaded at Chattanooga, it was done with the perjured and government-directed testimony of a man named Edward Grady Partin. He was in the can on a kidnap charge when he was let out by Robert Kennedy's Get-Hoffa Squad to entrap me. More on that later, too.

What I'm getting to is that I have an affidavit from Partin detailing the whole government conspiracy. It was brought to me by Audie Murphy, the World War II hero and movie star, as I began my fight to have my parole conditions lifted and knock Fitzsimmons out of office.

Murphy subsequently was killed in a private plane crash under suspicious circumstances, although eventually the whole thing was whitewashed and hushed up. But I keep wondering if he got it because he was helping Jimmy Hoffa.

Fitzsimmons came up under me but he didn't know the way things had to be worked. Actually he doesn't know his ass from first base about operations and hasn't done a thing to make any gains for the membership. All he did was get "Potomac fever" and join the country-club set. He didn't remember where he came from. He got up on the mountain and forgot that the members live in the valley.

When you run an organization like the Teamsters one man

has to be the boss and run things. I always had a lot of so-called advisers and counselors. But hell, you get a bunch of committees or something and nothing gets done. In the final showdown I did it my way.

I remember at one session I said we had a new contract. I'd made it. I'd approved it and I'd signed it. In the old days all you needed was a handshake. Nowadays you need forty lawyers. Anyhow, I'd signed the contract even though I knew there would be the usual gang of guys who wouldn't be satisfied, mostly just for the hell of it. So when I announced the contract a bunch of them started to yell and raise the roof.

"Hold it!" I said. "I signed it and this is the way it's gonna be."

Well, a bunch of them, maybe a hundred guys, tried to rush the platform. I'd expected this and my guys were ready for them. There was a free for all but we handled them. Contract approved.

So whatever happened while I was away can be laid right at Fitzsimmons' doorstep. And it will be.

Business Week magazine in its July 28, 1973, issue, had an article about "Jimmy Hoffa: On the Comeback Trail." It said:

"Knowledgeable Teamster sources speculate that Hoffa would have no trouble deposing Fitzsimmons in a rank-and-file election. Hoffa still is a labor hero to most older members of the International Brotherhood of Teamsters, who credit him with building up the union."

The article also said about my commutation restrictions: "Legal experts in and out of the Teamsters believe that the restriction could be successfully challenged in court. They say there is no precedent for such a prohibition."

They damned well said a mouthful there. I *know* I'm going to beat those restrictions.

In 1974 *Overdrive*, the totally independent truckers' magazine, ran a national poll of Teamster members. The question was: "If Jimmy Hoffa was eligible to run for the presidency of the Teamsters Union would you vote for him?"

Eighty-three percent voted yes.

They all know I'm back, very much back, and that I will be the general president again come hell or high water. I'm not a guy who believes in limited warfare, so the rats better start jumping the ship.

2
How It All Started

You almost had to live through it to really know the gut-ripping misery of the depression during the early thirties which led to labor's bloodiest and most violent days.

Prior to the stock market crash in October of 1929 people were going crazy investing [in the stock market]. Plunging on Wall Street was a fever in which millionaires were being made overnight.

Then came the crash. Guys without the guts to face the music jumped out of skyscraper windows. The bottom fell out of everything and as business came to a halt there were whole-sale layoffs. It got worse, and then even worse. By the mid-thirties we were a nation starving to death.

Entire families were living in city parks in huts made out of cardboard, tin, blankets, packing crates, or anything else they could scrounge. People picked through garbage cans trying to find something, anything, to eat. On street corners hungry guys sold apples for a lousy nickel and gobbled what was left. Thousands queued up in bread and soup lines. Hundreds of men, their bellies growling with hunger, lined up hoping for every scarce job no matter how little it paid.

Kids wore hand-me-down shoes, two sizes too large and

the holes in the bottom patched with cardboard inner soles. A slab of bread "buttered" with lard and, if you were lucky, seasoned with salt and pepper, was a luxury.

The whole country seemed to have lapsed into a coma. Crops from the Gulf to the Canadian border were ruined by drought. The nation's "bread basket" became a dust bowl.

Right here I have to tell you about the Hoffas and how I fit into the scheme of things. My forebears were among the earliest Dutch settlers in western Pennsylvania six generations ago and my great grandparents pioneered into Owen County, Indiana. My father, John Hoffa, was operating a steam-powered drilling rig taking deep core samples when he met my mother, Viola Riddle, and they were married in 1909. They lived in Cunot, Indiana, until my older sister, Jennetta, was born and then they moved into their own house in Brazil, Indiana, which was headquarters for the drilling company for which my father worked. It was there I was born on St. Valentine's Day, 1913, as were my brother Billy and sister Nancy.

We lived in a section of Brazil known as Stringtown, a colony of miners and blue-collar workers. Then, when I was seven years old, my father died after being sick four months.

"I'll have to be both mother and father now," my mother told us. "I'll have to work and you'll all have to help. It will be hard but we'll manage."

There was, in those days, no such thing as welfare, relief, or aid for dependent children. And I have a feeling that my mother wouldn't have accepted it if there had been. Certainly there is a need for judiciously handled welfare programs. But I hate to think we'll destroy our self-reliance and the independence that is our American heritage.

Some people have claimed that I carried a grudge against big business because of my background. That's not true. We had a rich and rewarding childhood and never felt deprived or impoverished. My mother was a quiet woman who believed in strict discipline, aided by a razor strop hanging in the pantry and a large bottle of castor oil on the kitchen shelf. But she was warm and loving and taught us the value and rewards of hard work. She knew what hard work was, too, cooking in a restaurant on Main Street and doing housework in the big houses on "The Hill." My mother also took in washing, Jennetta helping with the ironing while Billy and I did the delivering.

In 1924, when I was eleven, Mother moved us to Detroit because she felt that she'd have a chance to make more money there. She worked first in a laundry and then in an auto-parts factory on the production line, finally getting a job polishing radiator caps in the Fisher Body Fleetwood plant. She worked damned hard and always looked tired.

When I was twelve I began bagging potatoes in a grocery store every weekend for fifty cents and finally graduated to delivery boy, which meant a nickel and a dime tip here and there. In 1927, when I was fourteen and was to enter ninth grade, I had had it. I wanted to be a man and bring home some money. I went up to Western High School, sat there in the registration room until they reached the G's, and then got up and walked out.

"Mom," I said, "I decided to get a job."

"I'd like you to continue your education," she told me, "but you have to want to do it. It's your decision."

The next day I got a job at Frank and Cedar's department store as a stock boy at twelve dollars a week, ten hours a day, six days a week. I worked there two years, dreaming of becoming a clerk and, possibly, a part of management. It was a happy time.

But then in 1929, when I was sixteen, came the crash.

There was no more laughing among the employees. As the layoffs began people were scared, and with damned good reason. Like I said earlier, the bottom fell out of everything. Then a friend of mine named Walt Murphy made what I thought was a good analysis.

"Get into the food business," he told me. "No matter what happens, people have to eat."

It made sense to me, even though nobody could see right then how bad the depression was really going to get.

We had a boarder named Jim Langley, who eventually married my sister Jennetta, and he was a driver for the Kroger grocery chain. He asked me if I was serious about getting into the food business and said he thought he could get me a job at the Kroger warehouse. When I told him that I was, he took me down to their giant warehouse on Green Street to talk to the night foreman.

I was only sixteen at the time but Jim told the foreman I was eighteen and, because I looked strong, he took me on the 5 P.M.-to-5 A.M. shift.

When I reported the next night there were no applications to fill out and there weren't any personnel procedures to go through. You just walked in, got in line, and they handed you a number. The job included sweeping the loading dock, unloading the freight cars that pulled up alongside the warehouse with their loads of fruits and vegetables, loading trucks, or whatever else had to be done.

We were paid thirty-two cents an hour. The problem was that we only got paid for the time we actually worked during the twelve-hour shift and sometimes we'd sit around five or six hours waiting to be called. There also were long "rest periods" for which we didn't get paid. For a forty-eight-hour week we could earn $15.36, but the trouble was that we had to put in seventy or eighty hours to get in those forty-eight hours.

What made our situation completely unbearable was that we had a foreman who was a solid gold son of a bitch. Actually he was called "the Little Bastard" by all the men. This guy was a real sadist. He thoroughly enjoyed screaming out commands and then cursing a man and threatening to fire him if he didn't move quick enough. He was a little tin Jesus in the warehouse and the only time he smiled was when he had fired somebody. Nor, at that time, was there any appeal, any form of job security.

The oldest fellow in our crew was a man named Sam Calhoun, who once had belonged to a union, and he suggested that the only way to correct conditions at Kroger's was to organize and strike. Striking was against the law in Michigan at that time but that didn't worry me or Bobby Holmes, a youngster of about my age who became a lifelong friend and eventually an international vice-president of the Teamsters.

The history of strikes in Detroit during those years was a bloody one. Goon squads and strikebreaking crews could be formed overnight by managements from among the hungry and desperate men pounding the sidewalks and the workers were terrorized.

But we had a plan. Quietly we began to talk union with the night crew although we knew we would have to wait for exactly the right moment. The Little Bastard helped more than he knew. For early one morning in May of 1931 two waiting workers went outside to eat at a lunch cart. When they came back he fired them in front of the whole crew.

Even the guys frightened about losing their jobs if we went on strike knew that something had to be done. Some still didn't want to join in but we convinced them. It was suggested that it was better to be unemployed than to wind up in a hospital. You had to be tough if you were going to survive.

A couple of nights later the perfect moment arrived when several reefers—sealed cold-storage boxcars used to ship perishable fruits and vegetables—were backed in against the unloading dock. The boxcars were filled with ripe strawberries. Once the cars were opened and the strawberries were exposed to the air they would start to spoil immediately.

"This is it," I told Sam and Bobby. "If we don't go tonight we'll never go."

The word was passed around among the men to follow our lead. We waited until we'd unloaded less than half of the strawberries. Then I put down the crate I was carrying right in the middle of the unloading dock and walked down to the other end.

Those were the first steps I took toward the international presidency of the teamsters.

The rest of the 175 men in the crew put down their crates, too, and walked over and stood around me.

The Little Bastard couldn't believe his eyes. He turned white and then red and I thought, hopefully, that he was going to have a heart attack. Then he started screaming.

"What the hell do you guys think you're doing? Get back to work, God damn it, or every one of you bastards are fired."

"The hell with you," I shouted. "We want Mr. Blough."

Blough was the night supervisor. His office was inside the warehouse, some distance from the loading dock.

"Blough! Blough! We want Blough!" We set up a loud chant.

Blough appeared almost instantly, coming out to see what the noise was all about. He took in the situation at a glance.

"These bastards . . . ," the foreman started to shout again.

26

"That's enough," Blough told him. "Now, who can speak for you men?"

I had just turned eighteen in February and I'll have to admit that I was scared stiff underneath. But I stepped out of the group and told him I was the crew's spokesman.

"What's the complaint?" Blough asked me.

"There are a lot of them," I said. "We have a whole list. But we'll have to sit down and talk about them."

"All right," he nodded. "I can't get any company officials at this time of the morning. But if you'll get back to unloading those strawberries I'll promise you a meeting at ten o'clock this morning."

We accepted and, as we went back to work, the foreman walked past me and growled in a low voice, "Hoffa, you'll be sorry for this."

Blough was as good as his word. We met that morning and for several days afterward with people from Kroger's home office in Cincinnati. I had become our chief spokesman and I told them of the unreasonable actions of the foreman, about having to wait in the hallway with no place to eat and of having to wait without work and never knowing when we would be called.

Out of these talks we obtained a simple one-page contract which, in Detroit in that period, was a major achievement. Management agreed to work out a call time and guaranteed at least a half day's pay. They also set aside an eating room for the workers and deprived the foreman of the right to summarily fire any worker. They also agreed to recognize our committee.

The next thing I did was to bring the men on the day shift into our little "union." And in these efforts, and in continuing meetings with Kroger officials, I began to learn the basics of union work: that when you talk to workers you'd better look them in the eye and know what you're talking about because they pretty quick can tell a phony; that the higher up you go the more reasonable are those with whom you are arbitrating; that you must be specific in your demands and unswerving in your determination, and that there is a time to be adamant, a time to compromise, and a time to come to agreement.

The men had elected Sam Calhoun president of our group, with me as vice-president and Bobby Holmes as secretary-treasurer. At one of our meetings one of the workers introduced an organizer from the Teamsters Union. He pointed out that while we would pay dues to the local and to the International in the event of a strike we would be backed by the union and, more important, would receive strike benefits. I was surprised at the number of our people who asked for my opinion.

"I think it's a good idea," I told them, and we voted ourselves into affiliation with the Teamsters.

I was pretty naïve and didn't realize that my support for Teamster affiliation, and my work in organizing the men on the loading dock, had become a subject for much discussion at Joint Council 43. This was the most important Teamster unit in Detroit. Nor did I know that Ray Bennett, the head man, had his eye on me and my activities.

What I did know was that the Little Bastard had never forgiven me for the strawberry incident. He never let up on me, making it obvious that he was out to get me, and I began to get edgy. I've always had a quick temper and there were times I was on the verge of taking him apart. It finally came to a head when we were unloading crates of vegetables. He had been on my heels all night, nagging me and whispering obscenities.

Finally I'd had all I could take. He was right on my heels

and I whirled around and threw the crate on the floor at his feet. It split open and showered him with vegetables.

"All right, Hoffa, ya did it, ya dumb bastard," he roared triumphantly. "You're fired!"

"Like hell I am," I yelled back at him. "I quit!"

The very next day I got a call from Ray Bennett. He was a tall, thin guy with a brush haircut and I liked him right away.

"We've been watching you, Jimmy," he said, "and we'd like you to come with us as an organizer. There's no salary but you'll get a percentage of the dues from every new member you sign. It's no picnic, Jim. Organizers are being called radicals and Bolsheviks. The Chamber of Commerce is nothing but a tool for the big companies. Ford has a regular army of close to five thousand ex-cons and real tough guys on hand as strikebreakers. Any time there's a strike we union leaders have to be up front and the goons and strong-arm guys can be expected to try to knock hell out of us. It's low pay and dangerous but it's a job we have to do."

I didn't hesitate. "Count me in."

That's how I became an organizer for Joint Council 43.

My first job was organizing the rest of Kroger's workers. There were about four hundred in various other departments besides the loading dock and I got them all. And it was at Kroger's that I went through my first strike. It was a long one and the company, as all of them did in those days, sent a wave of strikebreakers against us. We had a number of knockdown, bloody battles and six times I was beaten up and my scalp was laid open wide enough to require stitches.

During this era in one twenty four-hour period I went to jail eighteen times while walking the picket line.

A big, tough police sergeant came up to me and said, "What are you doing here?"

"What do you think?" I retorted.

"Okay," he said, grabbing me by the arm and leading me to a nearby paddy wagon. "In you go."

At the station house the captain on the desk asked the sergeant, "What did he do?"

"He was going to cause trouble," the sergeant told him. "I got there just in time."

"Did he?"

"No."

"Well," said the captain, "release him."

The sergeant went back to the strike scene in the paddy wagon. I took a streetcar.

"What the hell are you doing back here?" the sergeant roared when I showed up.

"What I started out to do."

"Okay, buddy. Back in the wagon."

So there I was back in front of the captain again.

"What did he do this time?"

The sergeant was a company man all the way. "He was about to do something."

"What was he about to do?"

"He was going to start a fight."

"Did he?"

"Well, no. I got him first."

"He wasn't fighting?"

"No."

"Did he say anything?"

"Well, I think so," the sergeant said.

"Like what?"

"I . . . I don't know, Captain."

"Okay, Hoffa," the captain told me. "You can go."

I used my last two nickels to get back to the picket line. And when I got there I'll be damned if the sergeant didn't grab me again.

When we walked into the station house the captain shook his head disgustedly. "Sergeant, you got to wait until he does something. Then you can charge him. But, dammit, you can't charge him if he hasn't done something."

Then he turned to me. "Okay, you can go."

The sergeant stomped out and I turned back to the captain.

"Captain," I said, "the wives of the men on the picket line brought some lunch while I was being brought here. I didn't have any breakfast and now I've missed lunch. I wonder if I could borrow a dime for a doughnut and a cup of coffee?"

He grinned at me and handed me a dime. I used it to ride the trolley back to the picket line.

And would you believe it, an hour later I was picked up again—and fourteen more times before the next afternoon. Each time it was the same story. I was released for lack of specific charges.

In those early union days, as I was getting my feet on the ground, I had a partner named Owen Bert Brennan. He was to become the head of Local 337, the second largest local in Detroit. Bert wasn't too big, only about five feet eight and 170 pounds, but he was unbelievably tough. Bert was a fellow who loved to laugh and tell jokes, but when he got mad he could punch his way through a brick wall. Everybody in Detroit knew it, too, including the police.

One day when I was alone, I was picked up by two detectives and taken to the precinct house for questioning. These two guys were known to be bad actors who liked to work you over in private.

I didn't give them the chance. When the door closed and we were alone I beat them to the punch.

"I want to tell you guys something. Bert Brennan and I were talking about you this morning and if there's any rough stuff you're going to have to answer to both of us. You know

31

Bert and you know me. So don't start no crap with me or you're going to get hurt."

They backed off. "We don't want no trouble," one of them said. "We just wanted to talk to you."

"Well, talk without using your fists," I told them. "I know you guys are paid to work over union people but it won't work with me."

The message got around. I was never manhandled by the cops.

But it was different when you came up against strike-breakers and cops in a free-for-all whenever they set out to break up a picket line. At times like that it was Katy bar the door and every man for himself.

Not long after that incident with the two cops, after one such brawl I was arrested, convicted, and fined on a charge of assault and battery. It came about when we were peacefully picketing the General Tobacco Company for union recognition. Out of nowhere a bunch of strikebreakers, most of them armed with clubs, came charging down on us. The cops, who were always on hand around a picket line, just stood there and watched as long as the strikebreakers were getting the best of it.

One guy with a billy club took a swing at me that could have killed an ox. I ducked under the billy and went to work on him with both fists. I put everything I had into it and he went down bleeding heavily from the nose and the mouth.

Three cops came running over and two of them grabbed me and twisted my arms up behind my back until I thought they were going to break them. The third cop helped the guy up and, while the two cops still held me, this guy worked me over with the billy club. He laid my scalp open and damned near knocked me cold before the third cop finally pulled him off.

As I said, I was arrested for assault and battery. He wasn't, of course. Nor would they let me file charges against him. I had to pay a fine, and also pay to get my scalp stitched up.

That night the pickets built a fire in a vacant lot to keep warm. My brother Billy was among those standing around the fire when the son of the owner of the company drove up.

"Where's Hoffa?" he asked, getting out of his car.

"Over there," somebody told him, pointing to my brother.

The guy walked over to Billy and, thinking it was me, without a word whipped out a pistol and shot him in the stomach.

Fortunately the bullet didn't strike any vital organs and Billy got over a slug that was intended for me. And it was typical of the times that no warrant was issued for the company owner's son.

But the word spread through union circles in Detroit like wildfire. Before the night was over hundreds of other union members showed up at the picket line. There were a lot of hotheads among them. Somebody tried to set fire to the plant. There were a lot of rocks thrown through the windows and the company police huddled inside, afraid to show their faces.

The company came to terms the next day.

It went that way on virtually a daily basis as the months passed into years. It was one long picket line after another, more fights with company goons and strikebreakers, more bruises and more stitches in the head, and I was arrested so many times I lost count.

One afternoon in 1935 I went to union headquarters to see Ray Bennett and they told me he was in a meeting and I should wait. Pretty soon he came out.

"Congratulations," he said. "You've just been appointed business agent of Local 299. It's a big step up, Jimmy."

As things stood in Local 299 at the time his statement was

somewhat questionable. There were about 250 members in Local 299, the general freight group in Detroit, but most of them weren't working at the time because of a strike. No work, no dues. The local was more than ten thousand dollars in debt and its checks were bouncing all over the lot. Its office was small and dingy and the local was about to be evicted for non-payment of rent. I was supposed to get a salary of fifteen dollars a week from the local's funds. But there weren't any funds.

My first job was to get the working members interested enough in the union to start paying their dues. This wasn't too hard and soon I could pay myself five dollars a week. I worked and slept in the office, going home only so mother could wash my clothes and, occasionally, so I could get a solid meal.

But I was really happy with what I was doing and was so involved in my work that I didn't feel a need for money. I didn't drink and I didn't smoke. I dated a girl now and then but not too often. If you took them out more than once right away they started thinking third finger, left hand, and I wasn't ready to go that route. Then, too, organizing had become an obsession with me.

Absorbing most of my attention, as Local 299 slowly started getting back on its feet, was a plan to sign up more truckers. In those days there wasn't much over-the-road travel yet. Mostly it was intrastate trucking and horse barns. So I began to haunt the loading docks.

Drivers then had to load and unload their trucks as well as make their own repairs. It was slow work getting them to realize that they were doing three jobs and getting paid for one. But they liked what I said and soon we had three different companies striking at the same time. Every time we won a contract we were that much stronger than before. But in each case it was the same story: picket, fight goons and strong-arm strikebreakers and get locked up.

One day Bobby Holmes and I were discussing our problems in a restaurant, particularly the need for legal representation. A man sitting nearby came over and said he was a lawyer and was interested in our conversation. I told him we couldn't pay him much but we sure could use him. Which is how George Fitzgerald and I started a long relationship which lasted all the way through my tribulations with Bobby Kennedy and damned bad years in the federal courts.

Fitzgerald stuck with us all the way. When we got arrested, which was often, we'd yell for him and he'd come on the run and get us out.

There was a simple reason behind the harassment. Employers have controlled our system of justice for as long as I can remember. They contributed large amounts of money to the chambers of commerce, their manufacturers' associations and trade groups. And they were the ones who put people in office. The police departments and the courts were owned and, to a large extent, still are manipulated today by the big employer. So Fitzgerald had his work cut out for him.

So did I. Because my next big project was to go after the men who drove the big rigs that hauled new cars from Detroit to the dealers.

Those guys needed help, believe me. They were paid by the mile and if they had a flat tire or a breakdown they had to fix it themselves. Lost time meant lost mileage.

First I tried to talk to them at the loading docks but, like most everybody else in those hard times, they were afraid of management and of losing their jobs.

So I devised a new plan of attack. I hit the highways—

Route 2 to Buffalo, old U.S. 6 to Cleveland, U.S. 112 to Chicago, and U.S. 10 to the ferry at Ludington—to nail them at a truck stop or when they pulled over to the side of the road for a nap. Those guys were perpetually tired and most of them could have slept the clock around. So they had a trick of lighting a cigarette and then they'd fall right off to sleep and wake up when it began scorching their fingers. Usually they slept with a tire iron in the other hand. This was the middle of the depression and it was their defense against looters or hijackers.

After almost getting crowned a couple of times I learned to wake them up, identify myself, and jump back quick to avoid the risk of getting a shot on the head.

They'd freeze up or tell me to get the hell out of there, but I also learned to make my pitch in a hurry. It gave them a lot to think about as they tooled those big rigs mile after mile, and gradually we began to sign up those fellows in ever increasing numbers.

But the companies knew what was going on. One day I spotted a rig parked off the highway in a lonely stretch of road. I pulled in behind it, walked up to the cab and when I couldn't open the door I yelled, "Hey, you awake?"

The door shot open and two goons carrying blackjacks piled out right on top of me. I never had a chance. They beat me right into the ground. Just before I passed out, one of them grabbed me by the throat and lifted my head off the ground.

"That's just a sample," he growled. "Stay away from our trucks. Next time you're dead."

Brennan, Al Squires, Marty Haggerty, and some others also had begun using the same tactics of meeting the drivers out on the road. It wasn't long before they began running into the same situation, so we started going out in pairs. Two of us were as good as any two goons.

So the companies came up with another dodge. Whole truckloads of goons would follow a rig and, when the driver stopped, they'd wait in ambush for us. It made it tougher but we kept at it, and when they showed up we'd get the hell out of there as fast as we could. Not all of us were lucky. Some of our people were beaten so seriously that they wound up in the hospital.

Then the police got into the act. We were, of course, well known. While a rig could drive out of Detroit unmolested with a driver and two big, armed goons in the cab, we were stopped and searched at every turn. Anything that might pass as a weapon—a tire iron or a jack handle—was confiscated. And we lived in a blizzard of tickets for every imagined traffic violation.

But we were a special breed of bulldog. We wouldn't quit. And so soon we signed up enough members to call a full-blown strike. It lasted a couple of months and in the end the companies sat down at the bargaining table and we got the car haulers a pretty good contract.

It was a beginning that was to eventually produce results nationally for the Teamsters.

3

Jo

I was at home one morning in May of 1936 when I got a telephone call from Joe Wilder of the International Laundry Workers Union.

"What's up, Joe?" I asked him.

"I got a strike," he said, "and I'm losing it. I need help."

"Where?"

"It's on your way downtown," he told me, giving me the address.

"Okay," I said, "I'll stop by and take a look. Their drivers belong to the Teamsters. They've only got four, but they're ours."

When I arrived at this little laundry there was a hell of a lot of confusion going on. While I was parking my car I was approached by a police lieutenant who knew me. Which wasn't unusual, because I was known to all the cops and had been locked up by most of them.

"What are you doing here?" he wanted to know.

"I want to talk to Joe Wilder," I said.

"You'd better keep moving," he ordered.

"Hold it," I told him. "I want to see Wilder and that's what I'm going to do."

He just turned around and walked away and I went and found Wilder. "Joe, what the hell's going on?"

He told me the story quickly. "These girls have only been getting seventeen cents an hour. They don't get paid for waiting until the boss thinks it's profitable to run the mangles, so some days they only get a couple of hours' work. He got mad because they organized and he ran them out of the place with a shotgun. They set up a picket line and he started hiring scabs to break the strike. This morning the girls went over to the trolley line, caught the scabs getting off the streetcar, stripped off their clothes and chased them down the street stark naked. So of course the boss called the cops and it looks like there will be hell to pay."

But things had quieted down gradually and now the girls were walking the picket line again, with a whole bunch of cops standing around watching them. It was the usual procedure. Management called the Chamber of Commerce and the chamber ordered every cop in the precinct to the scene.

"Okay," I told Wilder, "we'll be here tomorrow morning in force."

I lined up about forty of our people and the next morning we showed up at the laundry. It was a signal for more police, this time mounted cops. My people joined the picket line and we were marching peacefully when the owner drove up in his car. I walked over to him.

"We'd sure like to get this strike settled," I said. "If we don't, we're going to get the Teamsters involved."

He started yelling, as if I were going to manhandle him, and I was locked up, taken down to the precinct house, and booked. Fitzgerald had me out in an hour and I went right back to the laundry.

I no sooner got there than the owner complained to the

police that I had threatened him. So they snatched me again and once more I wound up in jail.

The next morning I went back to the laundry again. They had set up a conventional picket line with two rings of marchers, the outside circle walking clockwise and the inside pickets moving counterclockwise. I dropped into the outside line and as I passed the women on the inside line I tried to give each of them a smile to encourage them.

Then it happened. I was looking into the brightest pair of blue eyes I'd ever seen. They crinkled in the corners when she smiled back at me. Her hair was shining blond and although she was small and looked frail she walked erect and proud.

I felt like I'd been hit on the chest with a blackjack.

I was looking for her the next time we passed.

"Hi!" I grinned at her.

She smiled back again. "Hi!"

The next time we passed I did an about face and jumped into line behind her.

"There's a man following you," I said.

"Why, Mr. Hoffa." She spoke over her shoulder in a voice that sent goose pimples up my back. "You'll lose your place in line."

"Hey, that's not fair," I told her. "You know my name but I don't know yours."

"Jo. Josephine."

"Jo what?"

"Poszywak."

Polish names are common in Detroit but I pretended to misunderstand.

"Say, Miss Jo Posey," I teased her. "I have to go get some coffee and doughnuts for the pickets. Will you help me?"

"Of course, Mr. HUFFA," she shot right back.

We dropped out of line and, going for the coffee and doughnuts, I knew one thing for certain. I was hooked. Just like that.

While we were waiting for the coffee, I made my move. "There's a great movie at the Orpheum tonight, Jo. Will you go with me?"

"Tonight?" she questioned me in her low, throaty voice. "That's pretty short notice."

I had a sudden inspiration. "Well, you see, in this business I don't get off whenever I want to. It's just that this happens to be one of my few nights off."

"When's your next night off?" she hedged.

So I told her a little white lie. "Gee, I never know. Maybe not for weeks. Maybe longer."

She didn't say anything right away. Then she said she guessed it would be all right, gave me her address and told me to pick her up at seven o'clock.

At this time, by scrimping and saving, I had a late-model Chevrolet. That afternoon I went home, washed and polished the car, and spent a long time polishing myself. My mother started to smile at me and finally said, "Who is she, Jim? Anyone I know?"

She caught me by surprise. "What?"

"Exactly what I said," Mom laughed at me. "You might as well wear a sign saying Jimmy has a special girl. Who is she?"

"Her name's Josephine Poszywak and she works in the laundry we're organizing. She's only seventeen and it's her first job. And, Mom . . ."

"Yes, Jim?"

"She's beautiful."

I guess mothers know instinctively what others have to be told.

Driving up to Jo's house at exactly seven o'clock, I tooted the horn twice. Nothing happened, so in a few minutes I tapped the horn again. The front door remained closed and I began to get uncomfortable. People rocking on porches along the street were staring, so I blasted the horn. Still no Josephine. Now I was desperate so I jumped out of the car and went up and knocked on the door.

It was opened by a motherly-looking lady.

"Good evening," I said. "I'm James Hoffa. Is Josephine in?"

She didn't smile or invite me in. "Good evening. I'm Mrs. Poszywak. Yes, she's home."

Still standing in the doorway, she called over her shoulder. "Josephine!"

Jo appeared and her mother disappeared into the house.

"Hi," I said. "Are you ready?"

She wasn't smiling. "I'm not going."

I was flabbergasted. "Not going? I thought we had a date. What's wrong?"

"I'm simply not going out with you," she snapped, and closed the door in my face.

I stood there completely baffled, then drove back to the office and tried to work. It was no use. All I could think about was Jo. Finally I looked up their telephone number and called.

Her mother answered. "Josephine has gone to bed."

Then she hung up.

"I'll be damned," I said, completely mystified, and decided I'd be at the picket line early the next morning.

She was already there and I fell in right behind her. "Hey, Jo, please tell me what happened last night?"

Her voice would have frozen hot water. "You tooted your horn."

"I what?"

43

"You tooted your horn. Nobody does that in my neighborhood."

"But I didn't mean any harm, Jo."

"Maybe not," she snapped at me, "but we live in an old-fashioned Polish neighborhood. There are things you don't do and tooting your horn for somebody is one of them."

I was desperate. "I certainly didn't mean to be rude, Jo. Honest. But I don't see any harm in what I did."

Her voice was sharp as a knife. "Oh, you! Can't you see that everybody would know I was going out on a date with a new fellow. When you toot your horn, everybody looks."

"I don't see no harm in that," I insisted.

"Oh, you don't. Well, it makes it look like I come running for every fellow who drives up and toots his horn."

She kept right on marching, shoulders set and head high.

"Gee whiz," I said. "I'm sorry, Jo."

There was no answer.

"How about some coffee when we break?" I asked.

Again there was no answer. But after a little bit her head turned and she said, "Okay."

We went for coffee and I suggested, "Jo, let's start all over again. How about if you go to the movies with me tonight?"

She was laughing at me now. "I thought you weren't going to have another night off for a long while?"

"Well," I said, "I went back and worked last night."

"Did you?"

"Yes. Now tell me. Can I call for you at seven?"

"All right. But don't toot!"

I started laughing but she was serious. "You have to come to the door and call for me properly. I'll introduce you to my mother and you'll have to sit down and talk for a while. Then we can go to the movies."

"But I already met your mother," I said.

"No, sir, you didn't," she lectured me. "That didn't count. You introduced yourself but you have to be introduced by me."

That evening I did it by her book.

Parking in front of her house, I went to the door and rang the bell. Josephine met me and took me in and reintroduced me to her mother.

"It's very nice to meet you, Mr. Hoffa," her mother said, just as if she had never laid eyes on me before.

We made small talk for a while and then Jo stood up and said, "Coming?"

It was real dark in the theater and I reached over and took her hand.

"Polish girls don't hold hands unless they mean it," she whispered.

"Well, I sure hope you mean it," I whispered back, holding tight to her hand, "because I really mean it."

Not long afterward the laundry owner sat down and signed a contract. This was in May of 1936 and Jo and I started to date regularly. We were married on September 24 in Bowling Green, Ohio, by a justice of the peace. Jo always claimed I owed her a honeymoon. We went on to Cleveland and spent two nights in a hotel because I was slated to go to Minneapolis on a special Teamster assignment.

There hadn't been anybody before Jo and there hasn't been anybody since. We had a lifetime together and that's the way it should be. Since the day we met on that picket line, Jo has been my whole life. Jo and our children and our grandchildren. My family is the most important part of my life. We were close before there were any problems. We have never been apart.

Jo and I were blessed with two children, our son Jim and daughter Barbara, and they never wanted for anything.

Young Jimmy was an athletic boy who played hockey and

football, in which he was All-State in high school. He went to Michigan State and when I heard he was playing football I was really upset.

"I didn't send you to school to get hurt," I told him. "I sent you to get an education. If you want to keep playing football go out and get yourself a job and send yourself to college. If you want me to send you, forget football and get your education."

Duffy Dougherty, the Michigan State coach, came to see me and asked me why I made Jimmy quit.

"Let me tell you something, Duffy." I laid it on the line. "If he got hurt, which almost all the players do, you just send in a substitute. But then I've got him hurt. I want him to have an education and I don't want him playing football."

Dougherty gave me a bit of an argument. But once I make up my mind I'm a hard man to change. I didn't. And I'm proud that young Jim took my advice and became a fine lawyer.

Barbara got the American Legion award in high school and became a top student at Albion College in Michigan. When she was seventeen, friends held a testimonial dinner for me in Detroit and raised three hundred thousand dollars. I took her to Israel with me, we met Premier Golda Meir and used the money to establish the James R. Hoffa Children's Home on one of the hills in Judea where they say John the Baptist was born.

"This will not be an institution for disturbed, misplaced children," I said at the dedication, "because there are no disturbed children, only a disturbed society."

Barb told me she was proud of that speech.

When she married Bob Crancer, a St. Louis businessman, I was, of course, the fond father.

"Understand one thing," I told him. "My little girl has never wanted for anything, and as long as you take care of her, okay. But if you don't, you'll answer to me."

I shouldn't have worried. Our kids and their families are like Jo and me. They'd rather be home than out running around. Young Jim and his wife, Ginger, and their two sons live just ten minutes away and are around all the time. And we spend as much time with Barbara, Bob, and their daughter as we can. I'm proud of all of them. Their heads are on straight and their feet are on the ground. We're more than family. We're friends, too.

Jo has always been my anchor and most of the time she's right, particularly about people, and who to trust and who not to trust. But I give her the needle about one incident.

Back in 1940 I decided it would be nice to own a small dairy farm, a good, healthy place for the kids. I ended up buying a place in Memphis, Michigan, for $6500. It wasn't much to begin with but I kept fixing it up. Jo didn't like it and kept telling me to get rid of it. So finally I sold it at a small profit.

Not long afterward they struck oil on the farm and what I had paid $6500 for became worth a quarter of a million dollars overnight.

You should see her blue eyes snap when I tease her about that!

4

The Rise to Power

At the end of 1936, after Jo and I were married, I was farmed out to Minneapolis to assist Farrell Dobbs in organizing the over-the-road drivers because of my experience and success in the Detroit area.

It was a sticky situation. Dan Tobin, then the general president of the Teamsters, was lukewarm toward Dobbs because Farrell made no bones of being an out-and-out commie. Nor did Tobin feel too certain that we should organize the over-the-roaders but insisted that we concentrate on city-based drivers. Since Farrell was a hell of an organizer and already had signed up most of the drivers in Minneapolis, many of the top Teamster officials convinced Tobin that the eventual gains were worth the risk of tying up with Dobbs despite his risky political leanings.

It was a ball-busting risk because Dobbs had a hard core of assistants that included Karl Skoglund and the three Dunne brothers, Vince, Miles, and Grant. All of them had the same communist leanings.

Later, as we moved into the war years, Dobbs and the Dunne brothers were indicted on charges of conspiring against the government. Dobbs and Vince Dunne were convicted and drew sentences ranging from twelve to eighteen months. Miles Dunne was acquitted. Grant Dunne had a nervous breakdown during the trial and committed suicide. Skoglund was deported as an alien who had conspired against the United States.

This is the same Farrell Dobbs who later became a top Socialist and ran for president of the United States in 1960 on the S.W.P. (Socialist Workers Party) ticket. He was an avowed Trotskyite who felt that a communist revolution had to be worldwide to succeed, as opposed to the Stalinists, who believed in conquering one country at a time.

Personally I've always felt that all communists were screwballs. It's my opinion that any ills in our system can be corrected without destroying our freedoms and the democratic processes. Then, too, I didn't like Dobbs' outspoken stand that unions should be a decisive political force. I couldn't buy it then, and I don't buy it now. I always have said in public as well as in private that unions should stay the hell out of politics unless a tremendous social issue is at stake.

Naturally, because I'd made it work in the Detroit area, I did buy Dobbs' theory that we should go after the over-the-road drivers, the long-haul guys. That way, too, we would be able to spread the Teamster message all the way across the country.

One of the chief supporters of the Dobbs plan was Red O'Laughlin, head of the Teamsters in Detroit. He decided to go to Minneapolis to hash things out with Dobbs. Because I had started working with the car haulers in the Detroit area he took me along with him. I mostly listened, but Dobbs made a point of milking me about the problems we had bumped into and the tactics we had used in signing up the car haulers. We'd only been back a couple of days when I was called to O'Laughlin's office.

"We're farming you out to Farrell Dobbs in Minneapolis, Jimmy," he told me. "He says he could really use your help in organizing the long-haul guys. Will you give it a shot?"

"Anything you say, Red," I said, and shortly I was on my way to Minneapolis.

In January of 1937, Dobbs formed a North Central District Drivers Council, taking in thirteen locals in North Dakota, South Dakota, Wisconsin, Minnesota, Iowa and upper Michigan. I was just short of my twenty-fourth birthday so I was really flattered when he picked me to head the Midwest organizational drive.

It was tough work and long hours because we had to cover all the highways out into the boondocks. By the spring of 1938 we had a total of forty-six locals in eleven states, bringing in drivers from Indiana, Illinois, Missouri, and Nebraska, and a few from Ohio, which proved the toughest nut to crack.

Dobbs now put the whole setup under what was called the Central States Drivers Council. The aim was to get a uniform contract for all drivers doing interstate trucking.

Getting a package deal wasn't going to be easy by any means. The trucking owners all were rugged individualists and the American Trucking Association, when we approached it, contended that it didn't have the authority to bargain for its members.

Our next move was deciding to settle on Chicago as the place to start shooting for an area-wide contract. The reason behind this was that Chicago was the key terminal city for all Midwest trucking routes. It took a lot of persuasion, and the threat of a general strike, but the companies that were involved finally appointed an Operators' Committee which was headed by a man named Jack Keeshin. He was a reasonable guy, one who could see the problems on both sides, and we finally worked out a Teamster contract which was binding on all of the companies. It was a hell of a victory for us.

What we got was a modified closed shop in which all truck drivers had to belong to the Teamsters; owner-operators were to be paid for equipment rental as well as to get drivers' wages; there was to be elimination of "lost time" for loading and other delays for drivers who were paid on a "per-mile" basis; 60 percent of the Teamsters in the eleven states were to receive raises immediately, as well as a minimum wage just under the rate then given to the highest-paid drivers; and there was the establishment of a recognized grievance committee of which Farrell Dobbs was to be the chairman.

If you want to know how far the Teamsters have brought the nation's truck drivers, consider that in those days the highest-paid drivers were receiving $19 for a seven-day week, sunup to sundown. With our first contract we got them $.48 an hour for a sixty-hour work week, which is $28, but that was only the beginning. As of now they get $7.83 an hour, which is $469.80 for a sixty-hour week. Why sixty hours? Because overall they want to work that many hours. As one guy explained it:

"What the hell do you want me to have to do, sit around the house all the time with the old lady?"

But their benefits don't end there. Under Social Security they get $338 a month at age sixty-two. Under the Teamster pension fund they get $500 a month starting at age fifty-seven.

In 1940, Farrell Dobbs decided to go back to his local and he resigned from the Central States Drivers Council. Mike Healy was elected president of the council and I was named the negotiating chairman. The following year I became vice-president of the council. After this we organized the Michigan Conference of Teamsters, a confederation of all the locals in the state, and I was named its first chairman.

But don't get the idea that all of our troubles were over. Things were still tough and getting tougher. In that year of 1941 we struck the Railway Express in a jurisdictional dispute and closed them down for a month. They tried to operate with scabs, the worst name you could hang on a strikebreaker, but we knocked them back. Then on the first of November, management sneaked in an army of goons. They were loaded into the delivery trucks, and coming out of the garage they drove in a circle around the pickets. When the trucks had us hemmed in, the goons poured out of the trucks, swinging baseball bats and billy clubs, and began to beat hell out of our people.

They weren't kidding. They were out for blood. Morrie Cohen was poleaxed and damned near killed. He needed 180 stitches to close the gashes in his head. A bunch of our people were hurt but we kept at it and finally won our demands.

Ike Litvak was a little guy but he was long on guts. He was organizing the laundries and they made a punching bag out of him. Finally he had a Mafia price put on his head—who knew the gangsters?—and for six months he was on the run, moving from one rooming house to another so they wouldn't catch up to him. But he didn't quit. Finally they cornered him in an alley one afternoon and a half dozen strong-arm guys were obviously set on beating him to a pulp.

"Stop, already," Ike yelled. "Let me tell you guys something."

They stopped and propped him up against a wall.

"Listen," Ike said. "You guys have got a job following me around and beating me up. But if you kill me you got no more job. Then you won't have nobody to follow around no more and beat up. So if you kill me it puts you out of work."

They bought it. Sure, they kept up beating on him. But not so hard. Even when the price went on his head they figured he meant more money piecework than as a one-shot hit. Ike was always bruised, but he was alive.

Around this time in 1941, and before Pearl Harbor, Dan Tobin, the general president, was a close friend of President Franklin D. Roosevelt. He wanted to show FDR that the Teamsters were solidly behind the effort to send aid to Britain and the other allies. So Tobin was really embarrassed when, out in Minneapolis, Dobbs and the Dunnes began making wacky pro-Russia statements in public. Tobin was forced to take action. Dobbs' Minneapolis local was put in trusteeship, giving control of the local to Tobin as general president.

Dave Beck, who was to become the next general president, was sent out to Minneapolis to take over but immediately ran into trouble. Dobbs was inflaming the members of his former Teamster local to drop out of the Teamsters, which at that time was affiliated with the AFL (American Federation of Labor). Dobbs and the Dunnes were using all kinds of underhanded tactics and propaganda to get members of the local to hook up with the CIO (Congress of Industrial Organizations) on the grounds that it was "more liberal."

Now, too, it came out that the CIO, whose overall strategy was to get workers of all kinds under one tent, was trying to run the Teamsters out of business in Minneapolis. Denny Lewis, brother of John L. Lewis and head of UCWOC (United Construction Workers Organizing Committee), came in there and started a big drive to set up a union of truck drivers and helpers in the area. He brought in high-pressure organizing teams and, moving on a big scale, at the same time began organizing against us in Detroit, Flint, and Pontiac.

We met them head on in a bloody summer in Minneapolis and St. Paul in which a lot of guys were hurt. For a change, union guys were busting each other's skulls. Through it all the members wore two pins, putting on a Teamster button when we were around and switching to a CIO button when those guys showed up. They were waiting to see which union was going to win the battle. You couldn't really blame them. They were scared out of their britches because they didn't want to get caught in the bloody middle.

The big blow to CIO hopes came when Dobbs, the Dunnes, and Skoglund were indicted on charges of conspiracy to overthrow the government. Losing their help knocked the CIO out of the box in the Minneapolis area.

But the CIO still wasn't finished trying to undercut us. Their stronghold was in Detroit and they were going all out after my haulaway drivers. Strong-arm goons were roughing up our organizers and I promise you we didn't take it easy on them, either. We were winning that war, too, when they pulled in their horns.

They withdrew because the Michigan State CIO Council got a lot of heat from the CIO's strongest union, the UAW (United Automobile Workers). Their council announced it was in opposition to raiding among workers involved in national defense production.

Walter Reuther, head of the UAW, never had endorsed those raids against the Teamsters. This meant that USWOC had a lot of organizing capital held back from them. When the cash didn't come up they lost a bunch of their strong-arm specialists. But, as I said, we practically had them licked anyhow when they took a powder.

The funniest part of the whole thing to me was that as a way of saving face when they were getting their asses kicked they claimed it was because they were being harassed by

Jimmy Hoffa's friends on the Detroit police department. What a belly laugh. Those were the same cops who for years had busted me and would just as soon throw me in the paddy wagon as they would a CIO organizer. Maybe sooner.

The UCWOC got its knockout punch when the CIO convention was held in Detroit in 1941. There was a near-free-for-all when the United Mine Workers led a movement to try to unseat Philip Murray as CIO president and get the post for John L. Lewis. Murray finally was reelected by an overwhelming vote and he laid it right on Denny Lewis, who naturally had been giving him a bad time. Murray was honest in what he said but it must have given him great satisfaction to take a swing at Lewis, politics being what they are on any level.

"The raiding against rival unions has got to stop immediately," he ordered during his acceptance speech.

Denny Lewis closed up his UCWOC office and moved to Washington. The raiding was over.

But there was a happy conclusion to all that smoke and fire. A large number of contracts were up for renewal with employers who had romanced Denny Lewis as a means of trying to bust our backs.

Don't think I didn't make them pay.

We forced them to come up with damned nice pay raises for our drivers. Which, of course, made all the double-button wearers toss away one of those badges. And you can bet it wasn't the Teamster pin!

Then came Pearl Harbor. During the following war years we could do nothing but try to consolidate and hold on to our hard-won gains. Everything was tuned to the war effort.

My work in Detroit, then in Minneapolis, and finally in the

successful battle with the CIO had attracted the attention of Dan Tobin and other high officials in the Teamsters. Tobin offered to make me an international organizer but I told him I was happy holding the line in my own area and trying to set things up for a big postwar effort. But as a reward for my work, in 1943 I was appointed one of the three trustees who examine the books of the International each year.

When the war finally ended and the restraints were lifted we were able to go back to our goal of making the Teamsters the single biggest union in the world. The Central States Drivers Council plunged ahead rapidly on all fronts, except in Ohio.

Our main goal was to get uniform contracts for urban and rural cartage that stemmed from interstate trucking. The companies were always looking for a way to beat the improved wage conditions we were winning. One dodge they came up with was to move over into Ohio, where we were having a hell of a time cracking the ice.

Take as an example a bakery in Chicago. They engaged in different types of trucking, using large vans to move big loads of bread to their warehouses and supermarkets. But they also used smaller driver-salesman trucks to make home deliveries or small-store deliveries.

Now when they entered into a Teamster contract in Chicago the contract was geared to big-city living costs. So they'd move their business offices to, let's say, a small town in Ohio. There they'd ask for a local contract. The chances were pretty good that the terms and conditions they'd get from a small town local would be a hell of a lot lower than they were in Chicago.

Now they'd start cutting wages and increasing hours in

Chicago. They'd claim that, even though the bakery still was in Chicago and deliveries were being made from there, they'd have to pay only as much as the contract called for in the small town where they had their headquarters.

It was a sweet dodge and you'd be surprised how many companies started picking up and moving their headquarters to Ohio, setting up offices there so they could enter into a local contract and avoid paying the higher scale.

If we took the employers to court we knew it meant a long legal battle and a lot of our members would be losing a lot of money until it was settled. So what we decided to go after was contracts which guaranteed uniform provisions for everybody involved in interstate business in the Midwest.

I was involved heavily in trying to crack the line in Ohio when it came time for the Teamsters International Convention at Los Angeles in 1952. And it was pretty cut and dried that Dan Tobin was finished as general president.

The International Brotherhood of Teamsters had been founded in 1903 with our first headquarters in Indianapolis. Cornelius P. Shea was the first president and served until 1907. That's when Dan Tobin took over, and he held the job for forty-five years. But by 1952 he had grown old and was ready to step down. Dave Beck, who started as a truck driver out in Seattle and had been the successful head of the Western Conference of Teamsters, was being touted before the convention as the man to succeed him.

A bunch of my friends in the Midwest and other places began pushing me to challenge him for the job. But I've always said that timing is vital whether you're in a strike, a fight, or an election, and I didn't think the time was ripe for me to run for the top office. Besides, Dave Beck was my friend. I made damned sure there would be no hassle over votes at the convention by announcing my complete support of Dave, and he was elected without difficulty. I guess it didn't surprise anybody that I was named ninth vice-president.

It was a nice step upward and I was happy to go back and take another shot at that situation in Ohio. As I said, those guys in Ohio were tough nuts to crack. The independent truckers were strange birds, a kind of Midwest Yankee. They were rugged individualists, independent as hell, and for a long time they couldn't or wouldn't see the advantages of tying up with the Teamsters. I finally found out that one guy, an employer representative named Landus O'Brien, was the key man against what we were trying to do. For some reason or other he hated my guts so I tried to work around him. But the problem among those Ohio guys was that everybody knew everybody else's business. You couldn't work out a contract with one without the others hearing all the details.

But if you keep beating your head against the wall, something has to give after a while, either your head or the wall. And finally we began to knock down the wall. Gradually the independents had fallen into line. But it wasn't until late 1952 that we got to the bigger employers and Ohio's contracts finally were brought up to Midwest standards with uniform contract provisions that protected everybody across the board.

Once we had this in the bag we went after the Southwest and the Southeast. In those postwar years over-the-road trucking had mushroomed throughout those areas. They weren't all that difficult to get because they were driving their rigs up into the Midwest and getting an earful from our members. Everybody likes money, so they joined up.

The South—Tennessee, Virginia, and the Carolinas—was the last stronghold of the diehards. We moved into Tennessee and overcame the opposition, but it wasn't until 1957 that we really put the Teamsters across in Virginia and the Carolinas.

But by that time I was up to my ass in a no-holds-barred brawl with the Kennedys, all of which developed because the Teamsters backed Dwight D. Eisenhower and the Republicans in the 1956 presidential election campaign.

The goddamnedest battle of my life was shaping up right in front of me.

5

The Spoiled Brat

All my troubles started one hot day in the summer of 1956 at the Detroit offices of Teamsters Local 299. I had no idea then how hot it was really to get.

I was president of Local 299 and was holding a meeting with my stewards. Then my secretary called from her office down the hall. She sounded upset.

"There are three gentlemen here who insist on seeing you immediately. I told them you were in a meeting but they say they won't wait."

"Well, who are they?" I asked.

I could hear her checking out their names. Then she came back on the line. "A Mr. Kennedy, a Mr. Salinger, and a Mr. Bellino."

"Okay," I said. "Tell them to wait a little while and I'll see them as soon as I finish this meeting."

We had just gone back to our discussion when all of a sudden somebody started banging on the hall door. It irritated the hell out of me because I'd told the girl I didn't want to be interrupted. So I jumped up and went over and yanked open the door.

Three guys were standing there and one of them, a fellow

61

with a big mop of brown hair, started to push past me into the office. I don't push easy.

"Hold it," I said, shoving him back with one hand. "Just a minute. Where the hell do you think you're going? I'm in the middle of a meeting with my stewards."

"It'll have to wait," the young brown-haired guy says. "We're coming in right now."

At this I grabbed both his arms and shoved him right back out into the hallway. "Like hell you are. You'd better just stay right out there until we're through."

"Do you know who I am?" he asked, getting red in the face and speaking real loud. "I'm Robert Kennedy."

He said it almost like he expected me to get right down on my knees. It might have made me laugh but by now I was starting to get as hot under the collar as he looked. My voice got pretty loud, too.

"I don't give a good goddamn who you are. If you want to see me you wait right out there in the hallway until we're through with our meeting."

By this time the half dozen stewards were on their feet behind me and one of them asked "What the hell's going on, Jimmy?"

When you spend your life in union work you're always ready for the worst. During my first year as an organizer I'd had my scalp laid open six times wide enough to need stitches. I'd been beaten up by police, company guards, goons, and strikebreakers two dozen times in one year. My brother Billy had been shot in the stomach by a company official and I'd seen a union business agent beaten to death by company goons. You get so you're always ready to take an eye for an eye.

Those stewards getting riled up behind me had been through the same mill and were accustomed to meeting trouble head on. It wouldn't have taken too much to set them off so

I had to get those three guys out of there before all hell broke loose.

Which was why, when the young guy with the big mouth crowded me again, I shoved him back into the hallway so hard he almost fell down.

"And stay out there," I said, slamming the door shut.

"Okay," I told the stewards. "Settle down and let's get our business finished."

It didn't take us long and the stewards went out past the three guys waiting in the hallway. When the last one left, the young guy led the two others into my office. Then damned if he didn't walk right past me and begin yanking open the drawers in one of my filing cabinets. I jumped him, shoved him away, and banged the drawers shut.

"What in the hell do you think you're doing?" I roared.

He saw I was red hot and ready to take a swing at him and he backed off.

"I've come here from the McClellan Committee to get all your books, records, and other papers."

I wanted to clout him. "You got a hell of a lot of nerve. If you want to talk to me you'd better sit down and mind your own business and stay the hell out of my filing cabinets. Now sit down! And who the hell are these other birds?"

"This"—he pointed at the fat guy chewing on a dead cigar—"is Pierre Salinger, our chief investigator. And this is Carmine Bellino, the committee's chief accountant."

Salinger, as it developed later, was one of the Kennedy troops in the long-range march on the White House, for he wound up as John F. Kennedy's press secretary.

"Okay," I said, "tell me what's on your mind."

I guess he thought he had to impress me. "Do you know *who* I am?"

I started building up another head of steam. It went against my grain for anybody to talk to me in that kind of tone, let alone in my own office.

"Buster," I told him, "I don't give a damn who you are. Just get it through that thick head of yours that nobody comes in here and starts going through my personal files."

"I'm Robert Kennedy," he repeated like it was a name that made him able to walk on water. "I am chief counsel for the McClellan Committee and I intend to go through your office and find out what's here."

I had to laugh. "You're kiddin'."

I was to find out later that whenever he was crossed he acted like a spoiled, vindictive brat. Now he just acted like a spoiled brat.

"Just who do you think you are?"

I've always had a quick temper and it began to show. "I'll tell you who I am and, in case you're interested, I don't care who the hell you are or who you think you are. But I'm president of this union and you're not going to get one single thing out of this office by trying to be a tough guy. Hell, you ain't playing with the girls from Vassar so can the bull and get the hell out of here."

His face got really red this time and he pulled at his necktie like a guy who was choking. I just watched him while he looked at the two guys with him. They didn't say anything and he looked to me like he didn't know what to do next.

I made up his mind for him. I pressed a button on my desk and three of the stewards came in. They got there so quick I figured they had to have been waiting right outside in the hallway just in case these guys meant trouble.

"Show these gentlemen out," I told them.

"Now hold on," Kennedy said. "What do you think you're doing?"

I had to laugh. "Well, you can either walk out or get thrown out. It's that simple."

It was pretty obvious that we had the manpower to get the job done. They left without another word.

"What was that all about?" one of the stewards wanted to know.

"Nothing," I said. "Nothing at all."

I couldn't have been more wrong.

I was to discover in the years ahead that Kennedy, if nothing else, was persistency personified.

He came back the next day and, when I told my secretary to send him right in, he slapped a subpoena on my desk. He sat down, knowing better than to head for my filing cabinets.

"What's this for?" I asked him.

"I want all your books, records, and other papers."

"Well, you're not going to get them," I told him. "Just hold your horses until I call my lawyer."

"Never mind your lawyer," he said, getting up and starting for the filing cabinets.

I got in front of him and held a fist under his nose. "You touch those and somebody's going to get hurt bad and it won't be me. So you'd better just sit back down there while I call my lawyer."

He sat down, watching me without saying anything while I phoned George Fitzgerald, my attorney. George's office was only a couple of blocks away and, after I told him what was going on, he said he'd be right over.

When he came in, Fitzgerald read the subpoena and handed it back to Kennedy. "This thing isn't worth the paper it's printed on. It's no good."

"What do you mean it's no good?" Kennedy demanded. "It gives me court authority to take the papers I want."

Fitzgerald shook his head. "It's no good and you absolutely cannot take anything out of this office."

Kennedy was as mad as a wet hornet and got pretty loud. "You'll wind up in court for this."

"That's fine," George told him. "We'll see you in court and find out just why you brought this subpoena here."

We did wind up in court the very next day. Fitzgerald told the judge that the subpoena was too broad, would have to be more explicit and would have to explain just what it was they wanted and why.

"Exactly what is it you're looking for, Mr. Kennedy?" the judge asked.

Kennedy looked like a guy caught with his hand in the till. "I don't know."

The judge acted as if he couldn't believe his ears. "What do you mean you don't know? How can I give you a subpoena without you knowing what you are looking for?"

"I'm tryng to find something," Kennedy told the judge.

"Well, you can't do it this way," the judge said. "I'll have to limit the subpoena. I'm sure that if you'll list the records you want that Mr. Hoffa and Mr. Fitzgerald will cooperate with you."

Fitzgerald wasn't having any of that. "Your honor, we don't intend to give up any of our original records. We will provide them with photostatic copies of any necessary items that are requested, but not the originals."

"That's fair enough," the judge agreed.

Kennedy wasn't satisfied. "I want the originals."

"Now let's be reasonable," the judge said. "These people are operating a business and I cannot order them to give you their original records. If you so wish, you may go to their office and compare the copies with the originals."

Kennedy pouted like a little boy. "No. I won't go down there again."

When we were presented with a list of the records Kennedy wanted, we got them together and had them photostated. There was a hell of a pile of them. Then I told Chuck O'Brien, one of my aides whom I had practically raised and who was almost like a son to me, to put them in a station wagon and take them down to Kennedy at the Federal Building.

"Make sure he signs for every damned piece of paper," I ordered Chuck, "or don't give them to him. I don't want some of them getting 'lost' and him claiming we didn't give them to him."

Chuck came back with all the papers. He was laughing.

"The guy damned near flipped his lid. He said he wasn't going to sign for every piece of paper. He tried to push me aside and take them but I brought 'em back."

So we were hauled into court again.

"What seems to be the problem?" the judge wanted to know.

Fitzgerald told him that we had insisted each paper be signed for so that Kennedy couldn't claim later that we had not delivered some of the records he had asked for.

"We're not going to take the time to sign for every sheet of paper they give us," Kennedy said.

The judge shook his head. "Well, then, Mr. Kennedy, it seems obvious that you won't get the papers. But it seems to me that if I was a lawyer and I wanted certain papers that were being offered to me then I'd be willing to take the time to sign for those papers. And if I was the opposing lawyer and you wouldn't sign for the papers I certainly wouldn't give them to you."

Kennedy looked so damned frustrated I almost felt sorry

for him. Almost. But finally he agreed that he'd sign for each of the papers.

O'Brien delivered them. Kennedy signed for them and took them back to Washington.

But that incident turned out to be the start of what was to become a blood feud. Maybe it didn't seem like much at the time, but I had stepped on a poison snake.

That fall I was one of the earliest witnesses called before the McClellan Committee. I'll talk about those sessions later. But it was at this time that we came to physical grips for the second time.

Kennedy was a great one for convicting somebody in the public prints. He'd make all kinds of charges and claims in real cute interviews with the press but then never back them up. So now he announced that I would be questioned on the same day they'd question Johnny Dio, whom he described as "a New York Mafia leader." The innuendo was pretty plain. Guilt by association, one of his favorite tactics.

Sure, I knew Johnny Dio, not as a so-called Mafia leader but as an organizer for the AFL United Automobile Workers. A year earlier, in 1955, Teamster president Dave Beck found out that Dio was organizing in our jurisdiction and asked me to see what I could do about it. Through sources in the UAW I set up a meeting with Dio and after a couple of meetings we reached an agreement that we'd stay out of each other's jurisdiction.

I've never been able to understand why the finger is pointed at us in the Teamsters—and only at us—that we knew mobsters and hoodlums. Mob people are known by employers and employers' associations much better than we ever knew them and employers always were the first ones to hire them. Mob guys had muscle, and where in hell do you think employers got the tough guys when they wanted to break a strike?

The Spoiled Brat

In the old days when we didn't have money to fight money we took ball bats and knocked those tough guys off the trucks. They sent the Purple Gang against us 'n Detroit in 1935 and it was a real bloody business of bombings and beatings. So we made it our business to get to know them. I've always been as tough as the next guy, and there are a lot more like me in union work who weren't afraid of the devil. We made our point. They could let us alone and we'd let them alone. We didn't join forces with them and we didn't take any mobsters into our ranks. It was simply hands off by both sides because we let them know they'd get as good as they sent; maybe more.

Anyhow, to get back to Johnny Dio. I don't know and I never asked about any of his business aside from his UAW association and how it was affecting the Teamsters. I'm no cop. As far as I'm concerned every guy's business is his own until the time when it starts affecting me or mine. So when I meet Dio again in Washington, while we're waiting to be called to testify before the McClellan Committee, I say hello to him and how are you, Johnny. And when it comes time for the noon break he says how about having lunch and I say okay.

We went over to a restaurant and were just about to be taken to a table when right behind me there was a loud voice which says: "Hey, you!"

At the same time somebody grabbed my arm from behind and swung me around.

It was Robert Kennedy.

I acted instinctively. I guess that's only natural when you've spent a whole lot of time in your life ducking blackjacks, billy clubs, and tire irons. Through those years I'd learned that if you didn't move quick you might not live to move at all. What I'm trying to say is that I move automatically when people put their hands on me.

My hands shot out and grabbed him by the front of his

jacket and bounced him up against the wall. Hard. As I admitted before, I have a quick temper and I was really hot.

"Let me tell you something, buster," I said, loud enough so that people all around were looking at us to see what the commotion was all about. "I'm only gonna tell you this one time. If you ever put your mitts on me again I'm gonna break you in half."

I shoved him away so that he bounced off the wall again. "Now get the hell away from me."

Dio, standing a few feet away from us, never changed expression. We went on to a table and never even talked about what had happened.

Anyhow, when I got back to the hearings, Senator John L. McClellan, who was the chairman, called me up in front of him.

"Mr. Hoffa," he said, "it is my understanding that at the luncheon intermission you assaulted the committee's chief counsel."

I didn't cop a plea. I told him exactly what had happened.

"And," I told him, "I'd do the same thing to anybody who treated me like that."

"I see." McClellan nodded his head. Then he turned to Kennedy.

"Mr. Kennedy, I'd suggest that in the future you leave the witnesses alone outside of these chambers. And now, if you please, let's get on with the regular proceedings."

But Robert F. Kennedy was a man who always made a big thing out of how strong and how tough he was, how he had been a football player or something at Harvard, and how he always exercised and kept himself in top shape. Nobody could ever convince me that it didn't eat his guts out that twice now, in Detroit and in the restaurant, I'd outmuscled him and made him look like a sucker.

I know it's true. Because as the hearings carried over into the next year I was approached by Eddie Cheyfitz, a lawyer who was a friend of mine. Eddie seemed nervous and a little embarrassed.

"Jimmy," he said, finally coming to the point after some small talk, "Bobby Kennedy would like to have a private meeting with you."

I was curious. "What about?"

"I really don't know," he told me. "But I said I'd talk to you and see whether you'd have dinner with him at my home in Chevy Chase."

I was sure, by this time, that Kennedy was a hard-nosed guy who was so spoiled all his life that he had to have his way in everything no matter who got hurt. The kind of a guy you had to be as nasty with as he was with you or he'd run right over you. But it's always been my theory that you keep the door open to your enemies. You know all about your friends.

Then, too, as I pointed out about Dio, strange bedfellows sometimes sit down and hash things out to their mutual advantage. I'd sit down with the devil himself if I thought something good might come out of it and I sure as hell wasn't afraid to face Kennedy whether he was alone or brought his whole damned private army. And, as I also said, I was curious about just what Kennedy might want.

Cheyfitz looked kind of surprised when I said, "Okay, Eddie, set it up."

I got there first on the appointed night and a few minutes later Kennedy showed up. He got right to it.

"I'd like to talk to Hoffa alone," Kennedy told Cheyfitz almost as if he was speaking to the butler.

"I came here to get some things straight in my mind," Kennedy said after Cheyfitz left the room.

"That's okay with me," I told him.

"There are a lot of things about you, Hoffa, that I don't understand."

"Well, there are a few things about you, Kennedy, I don't understand, either," I said.

So then he began firing questions at me like he was a district attorney or something.

"How much money do you make as president of the Teamsters?"

I looked him right in the eye. "Right here and now, under these circumstances, I don't think it's any of your damned business."

"Now look here, Hoffa," he said, getting that same quick red color in his face that I'd noticed before whenever he was crossed, "I'd like to keep this on a somewhat friendly basis."

"Me, too. *Somewhat* friendly."

He ignored that.

"Tell me, why didn't you ever go to college?"

"That's a long story," I said. "In a nutshell, my mother worked her fingers to the bone for us four kids after my father died when I was seven years old. By the time I was eleven I was working to bring home money to help out. When I was fourteen I went back to ninth grade and lasted just long enough to walk out and get a job in a department store. When I was sixteen I was working on a loading dock. We needed the money. We never had any silk sheets in our family, Kennedy."

He ignored that crack, too. "How did you first get into union work?"

"Well, as I said, when I was sixteen I got a job on a loading dock. We unloaded freight cars for thirty-two cents an hour, when we worked, and that was for a twelve-hour shift, 5 P.M. to 5 A.M. We had a bastard for a boss. We organized and I found out I liked helping people, not stepping on them. That started me in union work."

He kept looking at me like I was some kind of a bug under a microscope and what I was saying didn't seem to get through to him until I mentioned union work.

"That's one of the main things I wanted to see you about, Hoffa," he said. "I want you to tell our committee all about the racketeers and hoodlums who are members of the Teamsters union."

He made me tired beating that same old dead horse. I tried to be patient.

"Let me tell you again, Kennedy, there are no racketeers or hoodlums in the Teamsters."

"Well, then, tell me about your ties with the underworld."

He was starting to get under my skin. "Man," I said, "you gotta be crazy as a bedbug. How many times do I have to tell you that we don't, absolutely do not and never have had, any underworld connections."

Then, out of the blue, he got at what I figured out later was the real reason he wanted to set up this private meeting.

"I understand that you're supposed to be a very tough fellow."

It struck me funny but I kept a straight face. "Now I don't know who in the world could have told you that and, honest, I can't understand why anybody would tell you a thing like that."

His next crack knocked me flat.

"Hoffa, I'll just bet that I can beat you at Indian hand wrestling."

I hadn't heard anything so stupid since I was a kid and another kid put a chip on his shoulder and dared me to knock it off. I'd knocked it off by flattening the kid. But this from a grown man?

"What was that again?" I asked him.

"I said I can beat you at Indian hand wrestling."

I leaned back in my chair and looked at him as if he was crazy. "Kennedy, you must be some kind of a nut. I thought we came here to talk, not to play kid games. I don't want to hand wrestle you. Forget it!"

"You afraid?"

I couldn't believe he was serious but he stood up, loosened his necktie, took off his jacket, and rolled up his sleeve.

"Man," I told him, "you are really something."

"Come on, come on," he said. "You're not afraid, are you?"

Christ! I couldn't imagine a grown man seriously acting like that. But obviously there was only one way to shut him up. So I stood up and peeled off my jacket. I didn't even bother to roll up my sleeve. Meanwhile he had cleared a table and we sat down facing each other, put our elbows together, and locked hands.

"Whenever you're ready," I said, and it was all so damned ridiculous I had to laugh.

I let him strain for a couple of seconds. Then, like taking candy from a baby, I flipped his arm over and cracked his knuckles on to the top of the table. It was strictly no contest and he knew it. But he had to try again. Same results.

He didn't say a word.

He just got up, his face red as fire, rolled down his sleeve, put on his jacket, and walked out of the room.

He didn't even stay for dinner.

I'm damned certain in my heart that Robert F. Kennedy became my mortal enemy that night.

6

The Start of
the Frame-up

I am convinced that there was a long-range scheme among the Kennedys to grab the presidency of the United States and keep it in the family for a whole generation.

First it would be John. Two terms. Then it would be Robert. Two terms. Then it would be Teddy. Don't think it wasn't possible. Power leads to more power, no matter what your racket, and not only were they rich and influential but they were smart as hell, too.

Anything is possible in Washington. Watergate proved that. The Kennedys saw their big opportunity in the Teamsters in general and James R. Hoffa in particular and they grabbed it.

It started with the 1956 Democratic National Convention, at which Adlai Stevenson was picked to run against the Republicans' Dwight D. Eisenhower. The biggest surprise at that convention was that John Fitzgerald Kennedy, then a practically unknown young senator from Massachusetts, came within a few votes of snatching the vice-presidential nomination from Estes Kefauver of Tennessee.

Naturally the Democrats started to look around to see where in hell this young fellow had developed so much unexpected strength. It didn't take a genius to find out that his surprise support had come from conservative, anti-union Southern Democrats. They were leery about Kefauver because he had pretty strong labor ties.

Now this could have thrown a monkey wrench into all the Kennedy plans. Any Democrat who has hopes of eventually moving into the White House on Pennsylvania Avenue could never let it be said that he was the beneficiary of antilabor support. On the other side of the coin, he couldn't take the chance of losing the Southern conservatives, either.

The Kennedys had an out.

Only two of all the labor elements declared their support for Eisenhower and the Republicans. One was the Carpenters Union, which at the time was temporarily in the doghouse with the United Automobile Workers.

The only other union to declare for the Republicans, and by now the biggest and most powerful, was the International Brotherhood of Teamsters.

Eisenhower won the election but the Kennedys had the cutting tools at hand and four years to sharpen them for the presidential drive of 1960. The two unions which had backed Eisenhower and the Republicans provided them with a handy target that would bolster long-range support of the Southern bloc while also pleasing the Democratic hierarchy and its Northern liberals. They were in position to have their cake and eat it, too.

They started laying their groundwork even during Stevenson's campaign. Robert Kennedy began the spadework when he announced that after the election he intended to investigate the Teamsters and the Carpenters. Why just the two unions that declared against the Democrats? Why not all unions? Nobody ever asked.

It's also pretty damned significant that when the Carpenters subsequently regained favor with the UAW they immediately became a lost issue. They were back in the fold and the Kennedys didn't mention them anymore.

The Teamsters became the sole target for their long range political coup, a plot which was to gobble up millions of taxpayers' dollars and demand the services of just about every investigative agency in the federal government.

It has to be considered damned unusual that no other union was ever investigated.

At the time of the Republican presidential victory, John F. Kennedy was a member of the so-called McClellan Committee, headed by Senator John L. McClellan. It was known officially as the Senate Committee on Government Operations. Brother Robert was, by some strange coincidence, counsel for the committee.

It should tell you something that after the election the committee was suddenly renamed the Senate Committee on Improper Activities in the Labor-Management Field. And they zeroed right in on the Teamsters.

Their first target was Dave Beck, who had succeeded Dan Tobin as general president of the Teamsters. And they went at it hammer and tongs. In 1957 and 1958 alone the committee held 207 days of hearings to investigate the Teamsters. They listened to 1033 witnesses and filed 35,408 pages of testimony.

It was a witch-hunt, pure and simple. The Kennedys were thriving on the publicity and it became so ridiculous that Republican members of the Senate committee demanded an investigation of the UAW in connection with the Kohler Company strike in Wisconsin.

Robert Kennedy sent two men to investigate that situation.

Whitewash!

But meanwhile he continued his investigation of the Teamsters without any let-up, using the full-time services of 91 staff employees and 158 employees of the General Accounting Office as well as agents of the IRS, Justice Department, FBI, Treasury Department, Department of Labor, Federal Bureau of Narcotics, and the Naturalization Service.

As I said, their first move was to take the hatchet to Dave Beck. He was called to account by the committee for alleged personal-income-tax evasion. I would imagine that if you put enough agents to work on anybody, and did enough nitpicking, you'd be able to find some kind of irregularities in anybody's tax reports.

When Robert Kennedy got Beck in front of the Senate committee he accused him of just about everything from stealing a half million bucks in union funds to robbing poor widows. All they got him on was trivial charges. Like that he didn't report $1900 from selling an automobile to giving false information on income tax statements that he never saw and never signed.

It's typical of the Kennedys that it took them five years to get Beck before all the appeals were used up. When Dave was getting ready to go away he called me and warned: "Take it easy, Jimmy, and for God's sake be careful."

He didn't have to spell it out. They had thrown away the rule book when they went after him and they were going to try twice as hard to nail Hoffa's ass to the mast.

Beck took his railroading standing up. When they put him on the prison launch to take him out to the federal penitentiary on McNeil Island in Puget Sound he told them:

"Well, it's a nice day for a cruise."

When he got to the island the cons had made up a song

to let him know that prison life was going to be rough. It went:

> Big Dave Beck
> Was a merry old soul
> With a buckskin belly
> But he had no soul.
>
> He rode it wide
> And he made it rich,
> Just another con now
> The son-of-a-bitch.

So they got him. But personally I still can't see how tax fraud, even if he was guilty, fell into the jurisdiction of an inquiry into "Improper Activities in the Labor-Management Field."

Anyhow, when it began to be certain that Beck was going to be deposed as general president of the Teamsters it was conceded throughout union circles that I probably was going to succeed him.

The Kennedys had their ears to the ground. So now they jumped on me with both feet. I became the number one target for their hearings.

It was a persecution that Robert Kennedy really enjoyed. We were like flint and steel. Every time we came to grips the sparks flew. It made me mad as hell that he would call a press conference and make all kinds of ridiculous, unsubstantiated charges. They'd be splashed all over the front page. It was his favorite tactic: trying to convict me in the headlines. And the Kennedys had so much clout with the press that when he was proved wrong, or when I made a denial, it was printed back among the want ads.

One such incident was when he announced at a press conference that he would prove that the Teamsters were connected with known gangsters and that we were "completely dominated by racketeers and hoodlums." He even came up with a chart listing 106 names.

We threw the lie in his teeth. For we proved that:

Sixteen of those named had never been associated with the Teamsters.

Nine had only been former members.

Thirty-four were former officers or employees who no longer were with the Teamsters.

Eight were officers or employees who had been arrested but never convicted of anything.

Twenty-six were officers, agents or employees who had been convicted before they were employed by the Teamsters, some of those being convictions twenty years earlier.

And of our 1.7 million members, a total of thirteen had "records" for such "crimes" as disorderly conduct or for traffic violations.

Not one single time was our bill of particulars on this ever challenged! Harold Gibbons, who put our statistics together, summed it up in the affidavit when he said that Kennedy's charges were "a case of the mountain having labored and brought forth a mouse."

However, after Dave Beck was sentenced to two and one half years in prison and removed from office, and with me at the head of the line to succeed him, Bobby Kennedy started pulling stilettos out of his bag of dirty tricks early in 1957.

Enter John Cye Cheasty!

Cheasty was a lawyer who was sent to me by a mutual friend, a Miami attorney named Hyman I. Fishbach. Cheasty supposedly had special training in dealing with Senate investigative methods and I placed him on a two-thousand-dollars-a-month retainer. I accepted as a fact that lawyers supposedly adhere to an oath not to serve conflicting interests.

But what I didn't know was that Cheasty actually was no more than a spy in the pay of Robert Kennedy.

I think it's interesting to note that by this time I had squared off in those three physical confrontations with Kennedy and dusted him off each time.

I didn't realize at the time what I know now. Kennedy was a spoiled brat who thought he could whip every other kid on the block. I'd damned well shown him that I was one kid he couldn't begin to handle. He wasn't the kind who took his lumps, shook hands, and forgot something like that. He was a vicious bastard and he had developed a psychotic mania to "get" me at any cost.

Anyhow, he put Cheasty on me as a spy. Kennedy tried to pass him off as an "investigator." But I was paying Cheasty and for my dough, he was nothing but a goddamned spy.

In addition to setting me up like this, Kennedy had me put under twenty-four-hour surveillance by the FBI, which, of course, I didn't know at the time.

Not long afterward, Cheasty called me several times and asked me to meet him. Each time he turned over to me what proved to be worthless McClellan Committee documents. I had no indication that these meetings were being photographed by the FBI.

One night, after one of these appointments with Cheasty and another lawyer, I went back to the Dupont Plaza Hotel in Washington, where I was staying, and started for the elevators to go up to my room. It was eleven o'clock on March 13, 1957. I was just about to get on the elevator when five guys came up to me.

"FBI," one of them said.

"Big deal," I told him. "What do you want from me?"

"You're under arrest."

"Under arrest for what?" I asked him.

"Just come along with us," he said.

I started to get hot. "Like hell I will. I'm going up to my room and make a couple of phone calls. Then I'll go with you."

They started to close in on me.

"Hold it," I said. "Don't try to roust me. If you want trouble you can have a whole lot of it. Most of these people here in the lobby are my people. You guys make a fuss and we're gonna have one hell of a big fight."

Another thing I didn't know, and it seemed silly as hell when I heard about it later, was that Kennedy had the whole place surrounded by more than ninety agents. We *would* have had a helluva fight. But they backed off and I went up to my room and called my lawyer, Edward Bennett Williams. I told him what was going on and he said he'd meet me at the precinct headquarters.

Those FBI agents were waiting for me in the lobby and I went along with them. On the way one of them said to me, "You know we've got you dead to rights."

"You're full of shit," I told him.

"You'd better tell us the whole story," he bluffed.

He made me laugh. "Listen. You go play your games of cops and robbers but don't get cute with me. I don't have a damned thing to say to you. My lawyer will do the talking."

When we got to the station house there was Bobby Kennedy and his wife, Ethel, along with a whole gang of newspapermen. He'd made sure to tip them off even before I'd been picked up and was all set to milk the arrest for as much publicity and political mileage as he could.

"We finally got you, Hoffa," he said, loud enough for everybody to hear.

"You haven't got a goddamned thing," I told him, just as loud.

I was mugged, fingerprinted, and booked on bribery and conspiracy charges in the Cheasty "case." Kennedy was in his glory, giving the press all the "details" and using his favorite tactic of getting a conviction in the newspapers.

Then he gave the newspaper guys the clincher:

"If I don't convict Jimmy Hoffa in this case I will personally jump off the Capitol dome!"

When it came time for the trial in June of 1957, Edward Bennett Williams had as an assistant a black lady lawyer named Martha Jefferson. Joe Louis, the former heavyweight champion of the world, who later married her, came by the trial to see her. Joe was originally from Detroit and we had been friends for years. He didn't hide it.

Bobby Kennedy screamed that we were trying to influence the jury, which included eight black jurors. He overlooked the fact that his staff also included a black attorney. They were simply throwing out a bunch of face-saving garbage because it was obvious right from the start that Kennedy had a losing case.

Kennedy testified that Cheasty voluntarily came to his office and told him that Jimmy Hoffa had given him a thousand dollars to get a job with the McClellan Committee so that he could spy for the Teamsters. Kennedy said he had never seen Cheasty before but checked out his story and believed it.

That was a lot of crap but you almost had to feel sorry for Kennedy. My attorney, Edward Bennett Williams, was the total professional: calm, sure of himself, and very thorough.

Kennedy was easily flustered and, as Attorney General William P. Rogers said subsequently, "a man whose work was too amateurish to be useful in court."

At one point in the trial, Williams made a point.

"I don't quite understand," Kennedy butted in.

Williams knocked him right on his ass.

"I do not expect *you* to," he said. "I think the lawyers here will."

It tickled the hell out of me. I thought Kennedy was going to crap in his drawers.

Williams hit a home run early in the case when he brought out the basic lawyer-client relationship as one that meant I could assume that Cheasty, as my lawyer, was being ethical in doing his job.

I think they expected me to deny everything. So it knocked them flat on their ass when I frankly admitted that I'd hired Cheasty, told how much I had paid him, and said that thinking he was a reputable lawyer it never occurred to me to ask him how he came by the documents which I testified he had given me.

We also proved that I had hired Cheasty before Bobby Kennedy got him to agree to set me up.

There was no question, as I saw it, that a bribery charge was in order. The only thing is that it should have been brought against Bobby Kennedy.

It was an open-and-shut frame and the jury thought so, too. For on July 19, 1957, just one month after the trial had started, the jury returned its verdict.

"Not guilty on all counts."

But as I keep saying, Bobby Kennedy was a vindictive bastard and he took his spite out on poor Joe Louis for daring to appear at that federal courtroom in Washington and show his friendship for me. Kennedy turned his troops loose on the former champ and they hounded him for income tax evasion and even threatened to take him before the Senate Rackets Committee. Joe went through hell for a long time because, by Kennedy's screwy standards, by being my friend Joe had become his enemy.

In a further attempt to save face after the verdict cleared me of the charges, Kennedy told the press that we had manipulated selection of the jury in putting eight blacks on the panel.

It's damned interesting to me what Senator McClellan wrote about the trial and that aspect of it in a book he published in 1962:

> . . . the defense used several tactics which may have played a decisive part in the trial. A combination of these resulted in eight negroes among the twelve jurors—Hoffa's attorney used his challenges to exclude a large number of white jurors. . . .
>
> One juror had fourteen convictions on his police record, another had nine. Most of these were for drunkenness and disorderly conduct. Another had a son who was in jail on a narcotics charge, and still another had lost his job with the government because he had declined a lie detector test to determine whether or not he was a homosexual.

From that description almost any jackass would have to think that we had selected the jury panel instead of its having been called by the government. And you'd also have to believe that the government lawyers had no right to challenge the jurors.

Whenever the self-ordained Johnny White Hats fumble the ball, or get caught with their hand in the cookie jar, they always have an excuse to try to make it look like *they* were victimized. Forget the poor son of a bitch who was the real victim.

All I can say in looking back at that trial is that I would have been acquitted by any jury of any color. Kennedy was a new hand at rigging cases and his frame-up didn't hold water.

Anyhow, when the trial ended in my acquittal I did something I probably shouldn't have done. After all, Kennedy was determined enough to eventually rip out my guts without adding more fuel to the fire. But I couldn't help myself. I kept remembering that night in the precinct house when he was actually gloating over my arrest and how he had promised the newspaper guys that if he didn't nail me to the cross this time he'd jump off the Capitol dome.

I sent him a parachute.

I also sent along a one-word note. All it said, in great big letters, was:

"JUMP!"

7

Gangsters and the "Irish Mafia"

The McClellan Committee did only one thing. It put the Kennedys into the national spotlight, gave them tons of publicity at my expense, and paved the way for John F. Kennedy to become president. Outside of that it was a nothing, a farce.

I'm writing this book because I'm going to have my say, and I'm damned well going to say what I think.

They put Robert Kennedy on a pedestal just because he was shot. They call him a legend. For what? Somebody said it right when they called him "the runt of the litter."

Okay, so I didn't like him. Like him? Hell, I hated the bastard. He was a parasite who had to work for the government because he wouldn't have known how to make an honest living. He used a knife for a crutch and if it hadn't been for his family he wouldn't have made somebody a good law clerk. Sour grapes? Bullshit. A lot of other people thought so, too, as I'll show you right here because I think they're damned revealing.

Kennedy people try to make out that when Jack became president, he and their old man insisted that Robert become the attorney general. That's a lot of crap. The spoiled brat blackjacked John into giving him the job. Don't take my word for it. I'll quote you from a clipping in the *Miami Herald* of December 7, 1969, in which former Senator George Smathers talked about the appointment. It says:

> The senator recalled a conversation he had with Jack by the pool of his father's Palm Beach house shortly after his election.
>
> The future president told him that he didn't think he should appoint his brother attorney general. "Father thinks he ought to be in the Cabinet and Bobby wants to be attorney general. What shall I do?"
>
> Smathers said, "Why don't you make him an assistant secretary of defense? A young man with ability can make a name for himself in the Defense Department, which gets the biggest share of our budget."
>
> Kennedy thought it was a good idea but didn't want to suggest it himself. "Will you call him and tell him?" he asked Smathers.
>
> Whereupon a call was put through to Bobby and Smathers asked the latter if he didn't think it would be a good idea for him to take an assistant secretaryship in defense for the aforementioned reasons. A very cool Bobby asked if this was his brother's idea. Smathers told him no, it was his own.
>
> "Whenever I want your advice, I will call you," Bobby told the senator. "And you might tell my brother if he has anything to say to me he can tell me direct."
>
> In short, according to the senator's recollections, if history records that Bobby accepted the post because his brother and father insisted, it will not be correct. Bobby himself wanted that job and no other.

Damned right he did. And he got it even though former Secretary of State Dean Acheson told *Newsweek* magazine in August of 1970 that he failed when he tried to persuade Kennedy not to name his brother Robert as attorney general.

And, when the appointment was made in December of 1960 the *New York Times* said in an editorial, "If Robert Kennedy were one of the outstanding lawyers of the country, a pre-eminent legal philosopher, a noted prosecutor or legal officer at federal or state level, the situation would be different. But his experience as counsel to the McClellan Committee . . . is surely insufficient to warrant his present appointment." It was such a crummy case of nepotism that the National Democratic Committee was buried under letters that were 100 to 1 against the appointment. Which of course was water off a duck's back to the Kennedys.

Robert Kennedy was power-mad and publicity-crazy. I think he got his jollies playing God. He used the McClellan Committee as a tool to try to ruin me and, always the big "football hero," he said that going after the Teamsters was "like playing Notre Dame every day."

When he had us before the McClellan Committee he tried to make it sound like we were a Mafia "family." It was always "Do you know Johnny Dio?" Or "Do you know Cockeye Dunn?" Or "Do you know Tony Beck?" Boy, how he loved to throw those names around. Conviction by association.

He gave me a royal pain in the ass. Hell, yes, I knew Johnny Dio. I knew them all. I made it my business to know anybody and everybody who might try to break a strike or try to move in on us or who might be a threat to the Teamsters in any way.

I said it before, and I'm going to say it again: I knew guys in the Purple Gang in Detroit. We fought them with bombs and billy clubs in Detroit in 1935 and both sides got hurt bad. We made up our mind to meet them, get to know them, and work out an arrangement under which they'd stay out of our business and we'd stay out of theirs. I knew Johnny Dio. Dave

Beck sent me into New York in 1955 to sit down with him be-cause Dio was organizing for the United Auto Workers, AFL, in our jurisdiction. We got along okay and reached an agree-ment to honor each other's union territory. They say he was a big gun in the Mafia. How the hell do I know? I went to his house. I didn't see any machine guns or bodyguards.

They said I knew Moe Dalitz and that he was a big deal in the Mafia. Hell, yes, I knew Dalitz. I've known him since way back when he owned a string of laundries in Detroit and we threatened him with a strike. Those were the laundries Ike Litvak was organizing and where they kept beating the hell out of him. We finally got our contract. I said here earlier that somebody put a mob price on Ike's head. Did Dalitz have it done? Hell's bells, I don't know. People don't put ads in the papers about that kind of stuff. But I know we got the con-tract, a good contract, and the Dalitz laundries lived up to it.

The McClellan Committee kept insinuating that Jimmy Hoffa was wheeling and dealing with gangsters with the Teamster pension fund, which we started in 1955. There's over a billion dollars in that fund and Kennedy was always making loud noises that I was loaning money to hoodlums, although he never proved it.

Welfare plans in unions started at the end of World War II. John L. Lewis took it into the big time when he called the coal miners out on strike for a health, welfare, and retirement plan. The steelworkers followed and the automobile workers came next. Then in 1955 we negotiated the first Teamster pension plan as part of a Central States contract covering 100,000 workers in Midwestern and Southern freight. Under the terms of that contract every employer paid two dollars a week into the fund for each worker. As I said before, and I'll say it again, you don't just let that money sit there. You invest it.

Okay, so the committee says Hoffa loans it out to gangsters. Like, they say, Moe Dalitz.

Well, let me tell you this. Moe Dalitz was an officer in the U.S. Army. He's a casino owner approved by the Gaming Commission in Nevada. He's been on committees representing the voters under the governor of Nevada. So if Jimmy Hoffa is associating with a hoodlum, what the hell are they doing? You got to say that the Army, the Gaming Commission, and the governor all are associating with hoodlums. So who's to say who's a hoodlum?

Sure, we loaned money to build hotels and casinos in Las Vegas. So what? Las Vegas borrowers were good customers. Never a default. Of course we've had our problems. Show me a bank that never had a default. A guy borrowed some money from us to build a warehouse and he died. The warehouse went bankrupt. We took it over and sold it in ninety days with no loss.

There's no hotel or casino in Las Vegas that we had a loan with that was ever found guilty of skimming. And even where there were things wrong, the Teamsters weren't involved in the hotel operation. We did business with corporations and once the loan was made we didn't interfere with the operation unless there was a default.

To get the loan they had to submit a financial accounting and give us an audit every year. Financial experts investigated and determined which were good investments. A trustee could only recommend a series of, say, ten loans. When the experts came back with all the data we'd select, say, two of them.

There have been cases where we did lend money to businesses which, for some reason or another, were turned down by other banks. There was a hospital in Detroit which couldn't get a loan. It was represented by Martha Louis and we loaned them the money. Now it's a success and never defaulted.

There's been a lot of gab about us investing heavily in Florida. Any fool with half a brain knows how Florida real estate has shot up. Money is in land. Twenty-seven years ago I was on a fishing trip with two guys and we bought a hundred and eighty acres for thirty thousand dollars. That's less than $170 an acre. One weekend the one guy calls up and says we can get twelve thousand an acre for it. I tell him I just ate breakfast and I wasn't hungry. Hell, I tell him, wait a year and we'll get twenty thousand an acre. That's Florida real estate.

We financed two hospitals in Florida, North Miami General and Plantation. Both are tremendous successes and pay right on time. They put the rap on Cal Kovens. The building where I live in Miami Beach is the Blair House on Bay Harbor Island. It was built with a $2.5-million loan from the Teamsters about fourteen years ago. You couldn't build it today for $10 million. You couldn't buy the property it's on for fifteen times what was paid for it. It became a condominium and the money is paid back completely to the Teamsters. The Teamsters loaned the money for that building to a man named Irving Green. Cal Kovens was the builder. Green got sick and Kovens bought him out. But, as I said, it's all paid off to the Teamsters but they make it sound like we financed some ritzy gangster hangout.

Ask people in Florida who owns the big Castaways Hotel and the Miami National Bank and they'll tell you Jimmy Hoffa owns them. The Teamsters made great investments in both places. The loans were paid in full. There was even an investigation as to who owned stock in both places. The truth came out. I had no interest in either one.

Nobody ever tries to find out how much those Teamster loans were making in interest and how much money we were making for our members' pensions. I'll tell you one thing. It was a hell of a lot.

Everybody yells that Hoffa is the pension fund. Well, in a sense that's true. I established it. I also am a pretty aggressive guy and I speak up when I feel there's a good investment to be made. But I didn't direct all those loans they yak about. That's why we pay our experts.

But to hear Kennedy when he was grandstanding in front of the McClellan Committee you might have thought I was making as much out of the pension fund as the Kennedys made out of selling whiskey.

As the McClellan Committee hearings went on, Kennedy tried time and again without success to nail me for something, anything. Of course it was all aimed at the newspapers.

At one point he heard somewhere that some Detroit laundries had allegedly given some Teamster official $17,500 as a payoff to settle a dispute. Without any proof, he just up and charged that I had received the money.

Howard Balkwill, a member of the laundry trade association, testified that he had given the money not to me but to Joe Holtzman, a labor-relations counselor in his own association. Holtzman was dead.

Kennedy was there with his usual innuendo. "You believed that it would go to Mr. Hoffa?"

"Well, I wouldn't make that statement," Balkwill said.

So they had not one bit of evidence that I was involved.

Kennedy called me to the stand the next day. "There is a situation in this case where, according to the testimony, no hearsay whatsoever but the sworn testimony of yesterday, there was a payment made of $17,500, a payoff in order to get an intervention from a higher-up in the Teamsters. Then you intervened."

"What does that mean?" I asked him. "That I got the $17,-500? Is that what you are insinuating? If you are, I didn't get it."

Kennedy acted as if he didn't believe me. "You didn't get the money?"

"I deny under oath that I got it," I told him.

"You didn't get any of the money?"

"I did not. None of it."

So what happens. Like I say, he was always playing to the newspapers. The next day there was a headline in the Washington *Post* which said:

WITNESSES LINK HOFFA TO PAYOFF

I guess you'd call that impartial reporting, right? Balls!

But he couldn't fool everybody with his position and his so-called charm. It was pretty obvious to impartial observers that his insinuations were just so much malarkey. Like the time he was questioning Joey Glimco, president of a Teamster local in Chicago.

"And you defraud the union?" he asked Glimco.

Glimco took the Fifth, and I'd like to say that, while I never used it, it's a perfectly legal response.

Glimco said, "I respectfully decline to answer because I honestly believe my answer might tend to incriminate me."

"I would agree with you," Kennedy said. "You haven't got the guts to answer, have you, Mr. Glimco?"

"I respectfully decline to answer . . ."

"Morally you are kind of yellow inside, are you not?" Kennedy needled him.

It was Kennedy's kind of attack, making insulting remarks, and the kind of thing that caused Alexander Bickel, highly respected professor of the Yale Law School, to charge that the McClellan Committee "with Mr. Kennedy in the lead . . . embarked on a number of purely punitive expeditions involving relentless, vindictive battering of witnesses. Mr. Kennedy appears to find congenial the role of prosecutor, judge, and jury, all consolidated in his one, efficient person."

There was one committee hearing which some people found kind of funny—funny ha ha, not funny peculiar. That came one day when he was questioning Barney Baker, an organizer who was supposed to have many friends in the mob. And Kennedy loved to roll off those gangster names.

"Do you know Cockeye Dunne?" he asked Baker.

"I didn't know him as Cockeye Dunne. I knew him as John Dunne."

"Where is he now?"

"He has met his maker," Baker testified.

"How did he do that?" Kennedy went on.

"I believe through electrocution in the City of New York in the State of New York."

"What about Squinty Sheridan? Did you know him?"

"Andrew Sheridan?"

"Yes," Kennedy said.

"He also met his maker."

"How did he die?" Kennedy asked.

"With Mr. John Dunne," Baker told him solemnly.

It broke everybody up.

But Kennedy still had to try to tie me in with the mobsters.

It gave him another chance to use those names he loved to throw out to the papers, like "Cockeye" Dunne and "Squinty" Sheridan.

"Didn't it disturb you that Baker knew these kind of people?" he asked me.

"Not a bit," I told him. "It was his job to know anybody who might put a spike in our wheels."

Kennedy and his troops tried so hard to make us look bad that a number of times they made real horses' asses out of themselves.

Once was when he made a big issue about an office building on Fourteenth Street in New York City which was headquarters for several labor unions. Kennedy suspected that the building was owned by gangsters and sent investigators to check it out.

"What did you find out?" he wanted to know.

"Well," they reported, "it's owned by your family, the Kennedys."

Another time it concerned Pierre Salinger. As I said earlier, he was an "investigator." As it turned out he might have had trouble finding an elephant in a telephone booth.

Salinger brought in a real hot case against the Teamsters. He'd found the wife of a truck driver who said her husband came home every week with a short paycheck because he had to make a kickback to his Teamster union agent.

Kennedy jumped on it, of course. But he was glad to forget it when the truck driver appeared and told the committee he was keeping another woman on the side. And, after all, he did have to tell his wife something.

As many experts have pointed out, particularly after John had the balls to appoint him attorney general, Robert was a bumbling amateur in the courtroom. There was, as an example, the time he questioned a madam before the committee. He tripped himself up trying to explain the difference between a call house and a regular whore house.

"A call house is distinguished from a regular house of ill fame, sometimes known as a walk-in, by the fact that the clientele is a select one. Ah, a, ah, a house of ill fame, or a walk-in, will accept anyone who comes to the premises. Another, ah, another feature, ah, another feature of, ah, the call house is, ah..."

Even the members of the committee were laughing so hard at this point that Kennedy just gave up.

It was bandied back and forth at one time that Robert Kennedy was supposed to have said that he had the press in his pocket. I don't know whether he said it or not. But they mostly went along as if he did.

Before he ever got on my back he tangled with a guy named Roy Cohn and that case proved he always was a vindictive bastard. It started in 1953 when Kennedy went to work on Senator Joe McCarthy's Permanent Investigation Committee, and the only reason I bring it up is that down the pike it did have a connection with me.

When Kennedy got on McCarthy's staff, the senator's top assistant was Cohn, a New York lawyer. Kennedy and Cohn never got along and a couple of times almost came to blows but, as usual, the Massachusetts muscle man flaked out. When McCarthy named Cohn as his chief counsel in the middle of 1953, Kennedy got pissed off and quit.

It has to tell you something that later on, when Kennedy was attorney general, Cohn was indicted on perjury charges by a federal grand jury in an alleged stock fraud. Cohn blamed Kennedy and said in court that his mail had been opened and his phones were tapped by federal agents.

I can goddamned well believe that because he sure as hell did it to me often enough.

Then there was a bitch of a story about Cohn in *Life* magazine—another favorite bit of Kennedy strategy, conviction by headline. But Cohen didn't take it sitting down. He subpoenaed the magazine's files.

This is where Hoffa comes into the picture.

In the magazine's subpoenaed files they found a memo marked "Personal and confidential," from *Life* staffer Henry Suydam to managing editor E. K. Thompson. It said:

> Last Saturday I got a phone call from Bob Kennedy asking if I could drop whatever I was doing and come to his office. I did, and when I got there he closed the door and told me the following: in a back room was a high official of the Teamsters, a man who had been privy to the inner workings of the organization since 1953. He was particularly knowledgeable about Hoffa. This official is honest, said Kennedy, and also quite an idealist. The man had been working directly with Kennedy and in secret for the last 2 years. He was now so disillusioned and disgusted with the corruption he saw all about him, particularly as concerns Hoffa, that he had just about decided to make a public break with the union. Kennedy said he had suggested to this man that he make his break via an article in Life in the form of a personal expose of Hoffa. Kennedy asked my personal word that for the moment only you and I would know of this matter. Kennedy feels, perhaps melodramatically, perhaps not, that the man's life would be in danger if word leaked out of his intentions.

Who was this "honest" man who was such an "idealist"? He was Sam Baron, an avowed Socialist I had threatened to fire as a field director in the Teamsters' warehouse division because of alcoholism. Baron had been one of those who opposed my election to the general presidency. So it is highly questionable in my mind whether he went to Kennedy or whether Kennedy went to him.

Life's managing editor obviously took the bait because there was another confidential memo to him from Suydam a few days later which said:

> I told Kennedy of your interest and he is delighted. He makes the suggestion that the piece go into Baron's background and philosophy somewhat, to help explain his disgust with Hoffa and his motivation for breaking with the Teamsters. Kennedy believes deeply that this is not a case of "sour grapes," but of a man acting out of conscience and principle. Kennedy thinks the break will be understood in light of his total life in the labor movement.

Other memos showed that Suydam met Baron in a back room of Kennedy's office and that, while Baron told him I had rigged my election to the Teamster presidency he couldn't come up with any proof. Which resulted in this memo:

> The expose stuff sounds interesting but to me at least, pretty undocumentable and therefore probably very libelous. But the more personal stuff, on what Hoffa is like and how he behaves, sounds pretty good.

So what?

Just that Robert Kennedy, the Attorney General of the United States and a man who should have been dedicated to justice and not a personal witch hunt, was setting me up again to convict me in the headlines before taking me to trial. He was up to his old tricks, trying cases out of court.

For at that time I had been indicted on Kennedy charges that I had accepted more than a million dollars in illegal payments from a Detroit trucker.

The *Life* story, barely skirting libel and which Kennedy had arranged, appeared in July, 1962, between the time of my indictment and the time of my trial.

It wasn't ethical and it sure as hell wasn't legal.

But, as I did more than thirty other times when he arranged false indictments against me, I beat him in court and was exonerated of the charges.

The underhanded deal he had cooked up against me with *Life* magazine made me mad as hell. We subsequently took the *Life* material to the 1964 Republican National Convention in San Francisco and asked the platform committee to adopt a plank demanding congressional investigation of the attorney general's tactics to influence litigation that was pending against me. The Republicans did, and called for the investigation.

The following month we took the same action at the Democratic National Convention in Atlantic City. Nothing.

The Democrats were forced to take action when the Republican plank was announced. The House Judiciary Committee voted to investigate whether the Justice Department had violated any citizen's constitutional rights. Not Hoffa's rights. "Any citizen's." They appointed a committee headed by Representative Emanuel Cellar, a Brooklyn Democrat who was a solid Kennedy man.

What happened? Absolutely nothing. The committee didn't hold a single hearing.

What it all adds up to, as far as I'm concerned, is that you don't have to employ a bunch of hoodlums or carry a gun to be a gangster. There's a damned fine line between mobsters who take a man's life and members of a gang in power who rob a man of his reputation. Hell, I'm not saying I'm an angel, but when it came to dirty tricks I couldn't hold a candle to the Irish Mafia.

8

The Board
of Monitors

In September of 1957, two months after I was acquitted in the Cheasty case, delegates started to arrive in Miami for the Teamsters national convention. The major order of business was election of a general president to succeed Dave Beck.

Everybody knew I was the leading candidate.

Particularly Robert Kennedy.

He timed his moves perfectly and got everybody into the act in an all-out attempt to have me beaten.

On September 24 the McClellan Committee just happened to resume its hearings.

I was the first witness subpoenaed.

McClellan announced I was being charged with thirty-three "improper activities" and said that I was "unfit" to lead the Teamsters. (All thirty-three were dropped later.)

Secretary of Labor James P. Mitchell advised the delegates to take into careful consideration that the McClellan Committee had charges pending against me. (Those same thirty-three charges that were dropped later.)

Thirteen so-called dissident Teamsters obtained an injunction—in Washington—to stop the election on grounds that selection of delegates was rigged, an injunction that was vacated the next day by the Court of Appeals.

McClellan in the meantime sent telegrams to Teamster officials gathered in Miami telling them that most of the delegates "might not" have been chosen legally.

A New York grand jury indicted me on an old wiretap charge. (Of which I was later acquitted.)

On September 18 the AFL-CIO, with which the Teamsters were affiliated but which didn't want to get Kennedy looking down their throat, ordered the Teamsters to get rid of me or face expulsion.

Kennedy was taking every shot he could at me. It has to goddamned well make you wonder who was guilty of "improper activities in the labor-management field." All I can say is that the committee should have investigated itself and Robert Kennedy.

I think that all he did was clinch the election for me. He went too damned far. Our guys were starting to get mad as hell at all this pressure. When I got up to address the convention I laid it on the line.

"I have no fight with the McClellan Committee but when a congressional committee concentrates on a personal attack or misuses its power it can be dangerous for all of us.

"Something is wrong when a man may be judged guilty in a court of public opinion because some enemy or some ambitious person accuses him of wrongdoing by hearsay or inference."

You look at a movie and the "heavy," the bad guy, quite often is some drunken stagecoach driver or some big, mean truck driver. Well, let me tell you something. A lot of our guys may be truck drivers and you can make anybody mean by beating on them. But they're not stupid. Kennedy just pounded too hard, showing he wasn't the smartest son of a bitch in the world after all.

For on October 4, 1957, I was elected general president of the Teamsters with 72 percent of the vote.

In Washington, Kennedy at one of his grandstanding press conferences said that he was amazed that I had been elected. And what had been an obsession with him up to this point now became on all-out war with, as usual, no holds barred.

The first move came a month later when in November the thirteen so-called dissidents, under Kennedy's prodding, filed a federal court suit to kill my election.

"They'll get the evidence to throw Hoffa out of office," Kennedy told the newspapers.

Then on December 6 the Teamsters were expelled from membership in the AFL-CIO because they elected me president. It really made me red-assed. Because I found out that Kennedy had whispered in a lot of the ears at the top. They sure as hell were scared they would be investigated if they crossed Kennedy. The thing that really bothered me as a life-long union man was that it caused a split in labor's unified ranks. It was back alley politics by the Kennedys. They kept most of labor on their side of the political fence for the presidential drive ahead and the Teamsters still were the patsy that would satisfy those Southern antilabor conservatives.

At that same time in December, I was brought to trial on that New York grand jury wiretap indictment. The charge was that I'd put taps on the phones of some of our Teamster officers in Detroit. The big laugh was that Kennedy's investigators said they learned about this by bugging my phone. They were guilty of doing what I was supposed to have done. Anyhow, it ended with a hung jury.

The case was retried in May of 1958 and we could prove

that my phone was tapped and my office was bugged. In the meantime there had been a Supreme Court decision that evidence obtained by wiretap could not be used in the federal courts. But Edward Bennett Williams, my attorney, made the telling point when he said:

"You can't tap wires with one hand and prosecute wiretappers with the other."

The jury's verdict of acquittal was unanimous.

While all this was going on, the federal court had been hearing legal arguments by the thirteen "dissidents" challenging my election. Finally, in January of 1958, the court named a three-man Board of Monitors to hold the Teamsters in receivership for one year with me as "provisional president" while the issues were settled.

Martin F. O'Donoghue, a Washington attorney, was agreed on by us and by the plaintiffs to be chairman of the board. Godfrey P. Schmidt, a New York lawyer, represented the plaintiffs, and Daniel B. Maher, another attorney, was our representative. Herbert Miller was named counsel to the monitors, and I'd like you to remember that name.

It wasn't long before the Kennedy hatchet could be seen at work. O'Donoghue, who supposedly was impartial, and Schmidt began making a series of unsupported charges. They also demanded that I remove the leaders of certain locals, something I didn't have the power to do as long as a local wasn't in trouble financially and there were no complaints from the membership. Hell, I'm not saying we were all choirboys. But I will say that if you are you better not try to run a union.

Our man, Dan Maher, was outweighed two to one on the board but he was a smart cookie. He kept a detailed record of the board's actions and activities.

The Teamsters' General Executive Board waited out the year as well as another sixty days and then set a convention for March of 1959. But Schmidt petitioned the court to continue the monitorship "until the Teamsters can be purged of undesirable elements." Meaning Hoffa.

Small wonder they were desperate to keep the Board of Monitors going. In that year, the monitors had grabbed $350,000 in fees. O'Donoghue and Schmidt also billed the Teamsters for $210,000 as attorneys for the plaintiffs and another $17,000 for expenses. All in all the monitors cost the Teamster treasury a total of $700,000 that year, which is pretty sweet pickings.

Maher countered by filing his records with the court, along with an affidavit that O'Donoghue, the supposedly impartial chairman, had said he intended to remove me from the presidency and also was trying to do this by using information he had taken from union files when he formerly represented the Teamsters.

We took our case to the Court of Appeals, and then Sid Zagri, the Teamsters' legislative counsel, carried our fight to congress. His point was that if the recently passed Landrum-Griffin Act was designed to protect the rank and file of unions from undemocratic processes, then how was it that under that law the Teamsters were denied the right to hold a convention and an election?

It busted out on the floor of the Senate and the House on the same day. Two conservative Republican senators, Homer Capehart of Indiana and H. Styles Bridges of New Hampshire, and two liberal Democratic senators, John Carroll of Colorado and Wayne Morse of Oregon, all called for an end to the Board of Monitors. Their demands were supported in the House by Congressmen James Roosevelt and John Shelley of California,

Frank Osmers of New Jersey, Abe Multer of New York, and Elmer Holland of Pennsylvania.

This provided us with a lot of clout, as did the evidence obtained by Maher and Zagri which was presented to the Court of Appeals. The court ordered an end to the Board of Monitors and approved a new election.

We had the convention in Miami in the middle of May and again I was elected general president, this time by an overwhelming vote.

Kennedy screamed that he had been "betrayed" and that I had "bought off" John Cunningham, head of the tnirteen "dissidents" whose suit had caused the costly creation of the Board of Monitors.

In the true Kennedy tradition he simply made the charge in a public statement. He just said it, period. No proof. No charges.

Well, it was a goddamned lie.

He had lost a concentrated effort to beat me and he was trying to save face. Meanwhile, as time proved, he made his own payoff. Herbert Miller, the man who had been counsel to the Board of Monitors, eventually was named to head the Department of Justice Criminal Division and handled Kennedy's subsequent cases against me.

So now it started all over again. There was an indictment against us charging mail fraud in our Sun Valley project in Florida. We went to Orlando and Jim Haggerty, one of our lawyers, who had been head of the Michigan Bar Association, discovered a small box with an electronic device on it hidden in his room in the San Juan Hotel. We thought it was a bomb. The police emptied the hotel and firemen went to the room and disconnected the wires. It wasn't a bomb. It was a transmitter put into his room so we could be overheard discussing our defense in the case. Well, hell, we beat them again.

During this time, John F. Kennedy had announced his candidacy for the Democratic nomination for president.

The big scheme—get Hoffa and the Teamsters—was played to the political hilt. JFK even had the balls to say, "I am extremely glad that neither Hoffa nor his group is supporting me in this campaign."

Fat chance.

He and little brother Bobby had been proving for years that they considered the Teamsters second-class citizens. But, looking back at that crack, all I can say is that something stinks when a man who never worked a day in his life with his hands can put the knock on the largest single group of organized laborers in the country.

They were smart as hell, though. They had the rest of labor behind them because the other unions were scared to death that the Kennedys just might start investigating them. Not that they had anything to hide, mind you. But that kind of crap costs a union a hell of a lot of time and money just to defend itself. All it could cost the Kennedys was the taxpayers' dough.

Even though JFK was a front runner by this time, there were some people who thought that Lyndon B. Johnson might be able to put together a coalition and stop him. So John Connally, one of LBJ's supporters, came to see me and Connally asked for the support of the Teamsters in trying to stop Kennedy. I told him right out that they'd have to stew their own kettle of fish, that there didn't seem to be any way we could influence what happened at the Democratic National Convention.

As it turned out, of course, Johnson settled for the vice-presidential spot on the Democratic ticket with JFK. The Kennedys poured a ton of money into that election campaign, along with their usual hoopla and that "beautiful people" bullshit, and still they barely beat Richard Nixon. It's part of political history how maybe Nixon got a short count in some critical precincts.

The Kennedys were great for investigations. I've often wondered what would have happened if they had gotten the short end of the stick when the ballots were counted.

There was bad news for me, of course, when JFK won the presidency. Because that's when little brother Bobby demanded, and was handed on his usual silver platter, the appointment as attorney general of the United States. With this added power in the hands of the greedy little rich kid, it meant that Hoffa was in the soup worse than ever. Nobody had to tell me that he was really going to go after my scalp now.

I knew that my worst days were still in front of me.

But before I get to how things finally were rigged against me, I'd like to say that I never felt any great animosity toward John Fitzgerald Kennedy. He was only the beneficiary of his little brother's hate toward me. Nor did I ever have any hard feeling toward Ted Kennedy. So I felt bad along with the rest of the nation when JFK was assassinated in Dallas.

However, I guess I've made my feelings about Robert Kennedy pretty plain. That's why when Lyndon B. Johnson became president I could understand the way he felt about RFK. According to Robert Sherrill in his book *The Accidental President*, LBJ always referred to Robert Kennedy in one way. He called him "the little shit."

I'll buy that in spades although in that connection I wouldn't have called him "little."

9

Two Killings Averted

Following his appointment as attorney general, despite the nation's other legal problems I still was Robert Kennedy's number one project. By now he had failed three times to convict me but it was no secret that his "Get Hoffa Squad" was working night and day to nail my ass. It was persecution, not prosecution.

They kept digging away and in May of 1962 I was indicted on charges of accepting illegal payments from an employer in violation of the Taft-Hartley Act. I was supposed to have been paid off to settle a strike. It made no difference to Kennedy that a Detroit grand jury had investigated these charges previously and found nothing wrong.

Ten years earlier, Owen Bert Brennan, my longtime Teamster friend, and I had founded a truck-leasing firm we called Test Fleet, Incorporated. The business was placed in the maiden names of our wives, Josephine Poszywak and Alice Johnson, for legal tax purposes.

Commercial Carriers, Incorporated, a Detroit company which hauled new cars from factories to dealers, leased equipment from our Test Fleet firm. The Teamsters represented Commercial Carriers' drivers and the government contention was that the company was forced to do business with our firm or they *would* or *might* be faced with labor difficulties.

Which was a load of horse manure; just more government harassment. If I'd tried anything illegal, like giving favors to Commercial Carriers or taking a blackjack to them, all the other new-car carriers would have screamed their lungs out.

But Kennedy was getting prepared to take his best shot at me yet. As attorney general he didn't have to do his own work, so the case, even as phony as it was, had been better organized than some of the others he had brought against me. He put 150 experts to work on it, searching out every possible angle, trying to get me any way at all, legal or, as it developed, illegal. He had the troops to keep at it and he had the money, the taxpayers' money.

It was a case in which there were a hell of a lot of shenanigans, and they weren't ours.

The very first day of the trial in late October of 1962 somebody claiming he was a reporter for the Nashville *Banner* phoned some of the jurors, who weren't sequestered but went home every night, and asked what they thought about the case. Kennedy, fearing a mistrial, called James G. Stahlman, the newspaper's publisher, and asked him not to print the story. At first Stahlman agreed but then, feeling his paper's reputation was at stake, used the story and offered a five-thousand-dollar reward for information leading to the impostor's arrest.

Next one of the jurors, James Tippens, told Judge William E. Miller that "a friend" had said to him it was worth ten-thousand dollars to lean my way. He was replaced on the jury. Two more such approaches to jurors were reported to the judge. One involved a juror named Betty Paschal, who was dismissed though she said she had not been approached and had no idea what it was all about.

I swear to God that neither I nor any of my lawyers knew anything at all about these attempts.

But, from the way they'd been trying to get me for years, I didn't put it past the Get-Hoffa people to have set them up.

If that sounds farfetched, consider the testimony of a guy named Fred Shobe, which blew the whistle on the government's methods.

He was an ex-con who had been paroled from Michigan State Prison. He testified that he was threatened by Walter Sheridan, head of the Get-Hoffa gang, with revocation of his parole unless he helped them. For two years, under the direction of Sheridan's special Justice Department unit, he had gone around the country causing trouble in various Teamster locals and looking for evidence against us.

Shobe came to us and told us what was going on when his parole expired and they couldn't send him back to the joint again.

This was his testimony under oath on the witness stand:

QUESTION: Let me ask you this now, can you tell us whether you had discussed with Walter Sheridan a plan to frame Mr. Hoffa?

ANSWER: We discussed Mr. Hoffa, Mr. Bufalino, a defense lawyer, and Frank Fitzsimmons and various teamster officials at different times.

QUESTION: Was that made plain to you by Walter Sheridan—that the purpose was to get Mr. Hoffa?

ANSWER: That is correct.

QUESTION: And it was indicated to you that it made no difference whether he was—whether they used legal or illegal means?

ANSWER: Well, preferably if there was something found that incriminated Mr. Hoffa, well and good. However, if there wasn't, the feeling in the department was that Mr. Hoffa should be in jail anyway, and that if we had to resort to unfair tactics, well, that's where a person like myself came in.

QUESTION: And that is why they called you into service, because they wanted you like you described, "That's why they wanted me in the service, to frame Hoffa"—is that correct?

ANSWER: Well, to get him by any means, fair or foul. That was my understanding of the matter.

QUESTION: And you were directly told that by Walter Sheridan?

ANSWER: That is correct.

Shobe's testimony wasn't even challenged by the government.

Since one of the government claims was that Test Fleet might not have been set up legally, we called as a witness attorney Dave Previant. He testified that he had told us in 1952 before we incorporated that the Test Fleet deal was perfectly legal. He knew the applicable laws and repeated his opinion of our legality.

Then, in the middle of the trial, on Wednesday, December 5, some goddamned kook came right into the courtroom and tried to kill me.

He was wearing a raincoat and he walked right up to the swinging gates that separated the spectators' seats from the area for the lawyers, defendants, and jury, came through the gate, and moved in back of me. The first thing I know is that I feel somebody standing behind me. I looked around and damned if this crazy bastard isn't pulling out a gun. He aimed it right at me and began shooting.

I'll tell you there was a hell of a commotion. The FBI agents, the U.S. marshals, the judge, the jury, and everybody else started ducking for cover. Well, I wasn't going to just stand there and let the son of a bitch kill me. I jumped right at him, slugged him on the jaw, and knocked him flat.

When he went down, Chuck O'Brien, who had been sitting in the front row of the spectators' seats right behind me, jumped over the railing and landed right on top of him. Then a deputy ran over and, instead of grabbing the guy who tried to kill me, the dumb bastard started banging O'Brien over the head with his gun butt to get him off the guy.

It turned out that the guy's name was Warren Swanson, a drifter who had worked off and on as a dishwasher. He was nutty as a fruitcake, saying he had "a message from a higher power" to kill Jimmy Hoffa. They took him away for observation.

I was lucky. The poor bum had tried to kill me with a lousy air-pellet pistol. All I got out of it was a few welts on the back and the arm.

What we didn't know as far as the Test Fleet case was con-concerned was that even before I went to trial the government was setting me up for a subsequent indictment in case they blew this one.

For on October 8 I had a call from a guy named Edward Grady Partin, head of a Teamster local in Baton Rouge, who said he had to see me about problems in his local. I told him I was clearing the decks in getting ready to go to Nashville.

Partin called me again on October 18. He told me he was being hounded by federal investigators "because I'm a loyal Hoffa man." Partin asked me if he could come to Nashville to see me and discuss his problems. I told him it was okay with me.

Partin arrived in Nashville on October 22, the day before the trial started, and hung around like a leech the whole time. He was in court every day and came up into my suite every night while I was conferring with my lawyers. Partin was kind of like the furniture. He was around but you hardly knew it.

One night, though, he said he knew one of the jurors and he

suggested in a kind of offhand manner that it might be a good idea if he "contacted" the guy.

"Lay off that kind of stuff," Bill Bufalino, one of my lawyers, told him. "We'll have nothing to do with that kind of talk, so just forget it."

The trial dragged on for two months and the government hadn't been able to prove one damned thing. Now it was getting near Christmas and everybody wanted to get the whole stinking mess over with. So finally it was given to the jury.

At the end of the first day of deliberation the jury came back and said they couldn't reach a verdict. It was seven to five for acquittal and neither side would budge. Judge Miller sent them back for another whole day on Saturday and they reported they still couldn't get anywhere. So he sent them back again on Sunday and late in the day he brought them in and asked them if they could reach a verdict by deliberating longer. They gave him a unanimous "no" and he was furious.

Judge Miller was really impartial. The hate was so evident in his face that he couldn't keep it out of his voice. Before declaring a mistrial he said he would have another grand jury investigate the possibility of influence having been used on the jury. That should have told us something.

When I got back to Detroit I was interviewed and said that I felt Judge Miller had been prejudiced against me throughout the whole trail and that Jim Neal was one of the most vicious prosecutors who ever handled a government case. How the hell else did anybody expect me to feel?

That was the same James Neal, incidently, who in a 1974 interview with Jim Kincaid on ABC television was asked:

"What is your view of the government's ability ultimately to gain a conviction of anyone it is willing to pursue relentlessly?"

Neal replied:

"The only discomfort I've ever had with respect to the Hoffa matters center on that subject—I have had some discomfort with the thought that if the federal government pursues any man long enough and hard enough, it's very difficult for him to escape."

All I can say is, he oughta know!

So now what happened next? There was an undercover drive to prevent certain Teamster officials from being bonded. It didn't take us long to find out that pressure was being put on a number of bonding companies to steer clear of our business.

Several companies said right out that they didn't want to get into the crossfire between the Attorney General and the Teamsters. One bonding company executive told Teamster officials in Indiana, "I don't want the pressure."

The heat really was on them. The Manchester *Union Leader* went into the subject in depth, also Roger Mudd on a CBS news broadcast. The newspaper made some inquiries in the Boston bonding field and discovered that the Boston branches of three major insurance companies had been ordered by their home offices not to bond Teamster officials. Boston is in Massachusetts. So is the power base of the Kennedys.

I documented all of this and asked congress to investigate, writing to Senator Lister Hill of Alabama, chairman of the Senate Labor and Public Welfare Committee, and to Representative Adam Clayton Powell, chairman of the House Committee on Education and Labor, both Democrats.

I was spinning my wheels. Nothing!

It was obvious that Robert Kennedy still was at it, hammer and tongs, and it wasn't long before I knew it for sure. At Nashville they'd simply been getting ready to set me up in the other alley.

10

Chattanooga Choo-choo

I t wasn't long before we were back on the legal merry-go-round. Five months after the Nashville trial I was indicted there along with six others on May 9, 1963, on charges of jury tampering in the Test Fleet case as they laid the stage for their final crime.

Indicted with me were Ewing King. president of Teamster Local 327 in Nashville; Larry Campbell, business agent for Local 299 in Detroit; Thomas E. Parks, a Nashville funeral-home employee who was Campbell's uncle; Allen Dorfman, a Chicago broker; Dorfman's business associate, Nicholas J. Tweel; and Lawrence Medlin, who elected to be tried separately in Nashville on charges of trying to bribe juror James Tippens in the Test Fleet case, although Medlin admitted he didn't even know me.

Because of the troubles that had cropped up in Nashville we asked for a change of venue so that the trial would be held in Chattanooga. We knew that federal judge Frank W. Wilson, in Chattanooga, had been appointed to his post by Robert Kennedy, but my attorneys thought this would cause him to lean over backward in being completely fair.

Which proves how wrong you can be. For I was railroaded

117

in an out-and-out frame-up arranged by Robert Kennedy as the government paraded a string of witnesses whose stories were thinner than tissue paper. For six goddamned weeks they lied like hell and the whole damned thing was rigged from start to finish.

Our rooms were bugged, our phones were tapped, and our lawyers' rooms were broken into and their files were stolen. We finally had to hire armed guards with pistols to be able to maintain our records. It was hard to believe we weren't in Russia. All it brought from the judge was a shrug of the shoulders.

"This is a kangaroo court," my lawyer, Bill Bufalino, told me soon after we went to trial. "Jimmy, they're framing you."

And they did a hell of a job of it right from the start.

The shit started hitting the fan even before the trial actually got under way on January 20, 1964. The jury panel of two hundred names had been sent to three Chattanooga industrialists for "screening." The list then was turned over to the FBI to have each prospective juror checked out. They had the works: what each one did for a living, where they lived, their background, and their philosophies.

We were provided only with the names of the jurors and Judge Wilson refused us any other information. What we faced was a "blue-ribbon" jury of upper-middle-class residents unlikely to be sympathetic to the cause of labor and we had no way of telling who to challenge for possible prejudice. They struck off anybody who might be friendly to unions. Then, when one hundred additional jurors were called, we were told that copies were not available of the questionnaires they had filled out for the prosecution.

To top it off, Judge Wilson would not permit the defense

lawyers to question the jurors but insisted that he would do it himself. How the hell do you like *that* for openers?

As the government presented its case it tried to show that we had attempted to influence Betty Paschal, who had been dismissed as a juror at the Test Fleet trial.

King, president of the Teamster local in Nashville, was charged with having sent a trucking-firm employee named Oscar Pitts to see Mrs. Paschal's husband, James, a Tennessee state trooper. The payoff supposedly was to be the use of Teamsters influence to get Paschal a promotion.

Under cross-examination, Pitts admitted that he had approached King in trying to get his longtime friend, Paschal, a promotion; that King had not brought up any mention of the trial in Nashville; and that King deliberately told Paschal not to talk about his wife and the trial.

Pitts said that he had been questioned so many times by James Neal, the U.S. attorney in charge of surveillance over me and my attorneys, and Walter Sheridan, Kennedy's chief investigator, that he was confused and "scared to death."

Besides, he said, Sheridan had threatened him, "If you don't tell the truth I will get both you and your wife indicted."

King testified that he talked to Paschal only because, as a Teamster official, he was interested in trying to influence state troopers into a more friendly attitude toward truck drivers. He swore he had not even hinted to Paschal that his wife might be influenced as far as the Test Fleet trial was concerned.

We had an affidavit from Paschal, taken at his home before the trial, that he and King never had spoken "about talking to my wife." Now, in court, he testified that King did ask him to "talk to" his wife.

Under cross-examination, Paschal admitted he had never reported the alleged jury-fixing attempt, even when he was questioned in Nashville the day his wife was dismissed from the jury. Asked why he changed his story now, he said he had been under FBI pressure.

FBI agent William Sheets had told him, he said, "I could get in trouble and maybe be indicted," and also possibly lose his job as a state trooper.

There was more of the same: a supposed ten-thousand-dollar bribe offer to Gratin Fields, the only black juror on the Nashville jury, which Larry Campbell was supposed to have tried to set up through his uncle, Thomas Parks, the Nashville funeral-parlor employee.

Parks testified that Walter Sheridan, Kennedys' Get-Hoffa honcho, had promised both him and his nephew immunity if they would testify against me. Both of them denied the charges against them and it was brought out that James Walker, a Nashville patrolman who was the chief witness against them, had been working for Walter Sheridan.

It was pretty goddamned obvious, as one charge after another was refuted and the government witnesses stumbled all over themselves, that the government wasn't making much of a case. They did, however, seem to know and be ready for every move we made.

Small wonder. For we discovered that our conference room at the Patten Hotel was bugged, the telephones were tapped, and everything we said was known to them immediately.

I had no idea this was going on until one evening when we got together as we did every night in our conference room to discuss plans. Two of my lawyers, Bill Bufalino and Morris Shenker, and some others were there.

"What do you think they'll try to do tomorrow?" I asked.

Bufalino put a finger to his lips, "Not here," he said in a whisper.

I still didn't get it so I turned to Shenker. "I think they're pushing too hard. They're acting as if they don't have a case, which they damned well haven't, anyhow."

Morrie waved me to be silent.

Then I got it. They were all sure we were bugged.

I really exploded. "Well, I'll be goddamned. I'm not going to take this crap. Let's call Spindel."

"Shhh!" somebody said.

"Bullshit," I yelled. "Let's find out and let's make them knock it off. Call Spindel. Get him on the phone and I'll get him down here goddamned quick."

They put their heads together, whispering. Then Morrie said: "Okay. Go ahead."

Bernie Spindel was one of the nation's top experts on electronic eavesdropping. He had been indicted with me, and acquitted with me, of bugging those phones in the Detroit offices of the Teamsters.

We got Spindel on the phone at his home in Rome, New York, and he agreed to get down to Chattanooga as fast as he could. He said he'd ship his equipment by air freight from New York on Saturday, hop a plane Sunday night, and be in Chattanooga on Monday morning. He sent his equipment but then called to say he couldn't get a seat on a plane to Chattanooga either Sunday or Monday, so instead would take a plane to Nashville, get a rental car there, and drive to Chattanooga.

You don't think we were bugged?

When Bernie got to Nashville he was met by two FBI agents. They followed him all the way to our hotel in Chattanooga, picking up a further escort of FBI agents by two-way radio as they came into town until Spindel was leading a regular parade. Maybe they thought they'd scare him off, but they didn't.

Bernie, when he got his equipment set up, did find that we were being monitored and that there were two radio-equipped lookout posts in nearby buildings. Knowing he was coming, they pulled their bugs and taps, but he did record one whole day of broadcasts.

All of the information we collected was placed in a sealed envelope and given to Judge Wilson with a request that he determine whether it could be submitted into evidence as proof of the government's illegal activities in connection with the case.

We might as well have been talking to the wind. Wilson didn't even open the envelope.

You think that's the way to conduct a fair and impartial trial?

But then came the killing shot that was to nail me to the cross.

Edward Grady Partin.

And *Life* magazine once again was Robert Kennedy's tool. He figured that, at long last, he was going to dust my ass and he wanted to set the public up to see what a great man he was in getting Hoffa.

Life quoted Walter Sheridan, head of the Get-Hoffa Squad, that Partin was virtually the all-American boy even though he had been in jail "because of a minor domestic problem."

"I've dealt with a lot of informers," *Life* quoted Sheridan, "and until this guy, they all wanted two guarantees: nothing traced to them, and never call them as witnesses. Ed asked for neither one."

Small wonder, as it developed much, much too late.

Let's take a look at this "all-American boy" and his record, which was carefully kept from the jury by Judge Wilson and the government.

In December, 1943, he was arrested in the state of Washington for breaking and entering. Pleading guilty, he was sentenced to fifteen years in the state penitentiary, from which he escaped twice.

Freed, he joined the Marine Corps and was dishonorably discharged. He had been accused of raping a young black girl.

Becoming head of the Teamster local in Baton Rouge, he was charged by certain members with embezzling $1600 in union funds and he had been indicted on thirteen counts of falsifying records and thirteen counts of embezzlement.

While out on fifty thousand dollars' bond, he had been indicted in Alabama in September of 1962 on charges of first-degree manslaughter and leaving the scene of an accident.

One day before the Alabama indictment, he surrendered on September 25, 1962, to Louisiana authorities on a kidnapping charge, the "minor domestic problem" to which *Life* magazine had referred. He had assisted a friend in snatching the friend's two small children from the friend's wife, who had legal custody of the children.

When he was jailed on the kidnap charge, his fifty-thousand-dollar bond in the embezzlement case had been revoked by the bonding company.

On October 4, 1962, the father returned the children to their mother and Partin again was eligible for bail.

On October 5, 1962, he was visited in the Baton Rouge jail by William Daniel, an investigator for the district attorney's office, and the district attorney, Sargent Pitcher.

With them was A. Frank Grimsley, a Justice Department attorney assigned to the staff which was to prosecute me in the Test Fleet case starting seventeen days later in Nashville.

On October 7, 1962, Partin magically came up with another fifty-thousand-dollar bond as well as five thousand dollars' bail on the Alabama manslaughter charge and another five-thousand-dollar bond on the Louisiana kidnapping charge.

On October 8, 1962, a day after his release from jail and three days after his meeting in jail with Grimsley, he telephoned me and said he wanted to see me, a conversation later revealed to have been taped by federal agents.

On October 18, as I told about in connection with the Nashville trial, he phoned me with that garbage about discussing his problems. Then on October 22, he showed up in Nashville the day before jury selection began.

Which is how he got to be the spy who came to dinner, taking orders from Grimsley and reporting our every move at Nashville to the government attorney. His orders were to search out evidence of jury tampering which, even before the trial, Kennedy's troops were planning to "discover." I'm sure Partin's orders included his suggestion that he might contact his "old buddy" on the jury, which would have made us a sweet setup.

So this was the backbiting bastard who was the government's chief witness against me, the "all-American boy" with whose help they were going to put me away.

Judge Wilson aided and abetted him.

This Robert Kennedy appointee ruled time after time that Partin's character and criminal record had no bearing on the case and could not be heard by the jury. Wilson refused to permit us to establish what Daniels had proposed to Partin in the Baton Rouge jail. Wilson ruled that I had invited Partin to Nashville, and, when the government wiretaps were exposed which proved that Partin asked me to let him come to Nashville, the jury was not allowed to hear them. Nor was the jury allowed to hear Partin admit to the court that he had been planted in Nashville as an undercover agent for the Justice Department.

Wilson made a regular habit of sustaining government objections or, at best, ordering the jury from the courtroom so that he could hear privately some of our most pertinent evidence. He did this to the point that 60 percent of our evidence was given in the jury's absence—and never was heard by the jury.

And each and every time we offered evidence proving government intimidation and subornation of witnesses, Judge Wilson refused to let it be given in the presence of the jurors.

Then when Partin took the stand, Judge Wilson ruled that we could not go into his criminal record. Which stopped us cold from trying to prove his extreme lack of credibility.

Edward Grady Partin was a big, rugged guy who could charm a snake off a rock. They brought him off to the jury as an honest Teamster official turned government witness because of his "disillusion" with the conduct of general president Jimmy Hoffa. And Judge Wilson's rulings let the government set him up as a witness who had appeared voluntarily—after Nashville—without pay or favor.

Perjury, in the eyes of the Justice Department, obviously depended on who was telling the lies. For when Walter Sheridan was on the witness stand he gave this testimony:

QUESTION: Have you ever authorized any payment to Mr. Partin?
ANSWER: No, sir.

QUESTION: Has there been, to your knowledge, any money paid to Mr. Partin?

ANSWER: No, sir.

QUESTION: Has any promise been made to Mr. Partin?

ANSWER: No, sir.

Yet there was in government files a July 3, 1963, memo from Sheridan to S. A. Andretta, an administrative assistant to the Attorney General, which set up a secret three-hundred-dollar-a-month payment for Partin, listed as a "confidential source," and which was paid to Partin's wife by Grimsley.

Informed of this—again when the jury first had been cleared from the courtroom—Judge Wilson found it of no special significance.

Christ!

Of course Judge Wilson permitted Partin to testify in front of the jury—overruling repeated objections by my attorneys—and my defense went down the drain when he said that I was "desperately" intent on rigging the Nashville jury and that I had told him I would pay twenty thousand dollars or "whatever it cost" to "get to" the jury.

Jim Haggerty, one of my attorneys, charged Wilson with gross misconduct of the case from start to finish.

"In my forty-one years of experience, mostly in federal courts, I have never witnessed such an exhibition," he said. "It leaves me clearly puzzled and somewhat disgusted."

I didn't find it too puzzling. Robert Kennedy finally had bought and rigged the thing he had been after for so long. I wasn't the least bit surprised that the jury found me guilty of the jury-tampering charge. A band of angels couldn't have beaten that frame-up.

On March 12, 1964, Judge Wilson sentenced me to eight

years in the federal penitentiary and fined me ten thousand dollars.

Three co-defendants allegedly involved with me, Ewing King, Larry Campbell, and Thomas Parks, also were found guilty. They each were sentenced to three years and fined five thousand dollars.

Looking back at the way the government rigged it, all I can say is that I was not guilty of the charge and that I was railroaded by the arrogant and ruthless bastard who never would have had the power to pull it off if he hadn't been Jack Kennedy's spoiled little brother.

At a victory party in Washington, the Get-Hoffa Squad presented Kennedy with a leather wallet embossed with the words the jury foreman said when he announced the guilty verdict. They should have put a bill inside for the $12 million his hatred had cost the government in the nine years it took him to "get" me.

And if you're a thinking American it has to give you a cold chill to know that the "Justice" department could do the same thing to you if you ever happened to cross the wrong guy.

11

You Can't Beat City Hall

They still weren't finished with me after getting that rigged conviction in Chattanooga. Kennedy played it to the hilt, milking all the press mileage out of it he could, and afterward I was brought to trial in Chicago with seven others on charges of fraud in connection with loans made by the pension fund.

We didn't have a prayer. On the basis of the Chattanooga frame-up we went in already convicted. For again there was a planned newspaper and magazine campaign against me and again the Justice Department used unbelievable tactics. Christ, they'd have hung the Twelve Apostles.

I'll let it go by saying that I was ordered to serve a concurrent five years and fined another ten thousand dollars.

There were now a lot of rumors flying around that because of these convictions the Teamsters' executive board would make a move to oust me from office. They were squelched in a hurry. The board met and gave me a unanimous vote of confidence.

And the Kennedy troops didn't have me yet either, by God. We fought them in and out of the Supreme Court for three years and—if we'd had the evidence we have now—we'd sure as hell have whipped their asses.

Anyhow, the Chattanooga railroading job was the chief cause for both convictions and it bounced back and forth in the courts month after month. Finally, the Supreme Court reviewed the case in 1966. Justices Byron White and Abe Fortas withdrew and seven justices narrowed the issue to whether Edward Grady Partin's role as an informer had violated my constitutional rights or whether it "constituted a reasonable step to protect the integrity of the jury."

In December, 1966, the Supreme Court upheld the jury-tampering conviction—based strictly on Partin's perjury.

Chief Justice Earl Warren dissented, saying:

> In this case, the testimony concerning the circumstances surrounding Partin's entry into Hoffa's councils was not substantially in dispute. While those circumstances are set forth in greater detail, a brief summary discloses that Partin, after discussing Hoffa with federal agents and learning of their intense and mutually beneficial interest, successfully solicited an invitation to meet with Hoffa. Partin's release from jail was assisted by the federal agents, and he was compensated in a financial sense as well; in return, he kept the federal agents fully informed of all that occurred from the outset of his contact with Hoffa.
>
> Surely the only reasonable construction of these facts is that Partin was acting as a paid federal informer when he traveled to Nashville and attached himself to Hoffa. And the fact that Hoffa on Partin's urging agreed to a meeting in Nashville is not inconsistent with the conclusion. An invasion of basic rights made possible by prevailing upon friendship with the victim is no less proscribed than an invasion accomplished by force.

In other words, I'd been set up.

So now we offered a one-hundred-thousand-dollar reward to anyone who could prove that our conference room in Chattanooga had been bugged and the phones had been tapped while I was conferring with my attorneys. A man named Benjamin (Bud) Nichols appeared and said he had been paid two hundred dollars to install the bugs and tap the lines.

This is what the *Wall Street Journal* said in a front-page story:

> Bud Nichols swears that Walter Sheridan, former head of the Justice Department's "Hoffa Squad," instructed him to slip tiny transmitters under the mattresses of the Chattanooga jurors when they were sequestered in the Reed House hostelry there. Moreover Mr. Nichols is prepared to swear that he placed four microphone "bugs" and tapped six telephone lines leading to rooms in the Patten Hotel which were occupied during the trial by Mr. Hoffa and his legal counselors.

Based on this, we filed a new motion with the Supreme Court at the end of January in 1967.

In the meantime, Cartha DeLoach, assistant director of the FBI, was quoted by reporters as having said that there was a special wiretap unit in the Justice Department and that Kennedy had ordered a three-man wiretap team to do a job on me at Chattanooga. DeLoach subsequently denied he had said it. The reporters dared him to take a lie-detector test. No dice.

But all this did give us enough to petition the U.S. Court of Appeals for a new trial and to ask the Supreme Court to review their earlier decision upholding the Chattanooga conviction.

But finally time ran out on me. The Supreme Court announced on February 28, 1967, that it would not reconsider its decision.

Forty-eight hours later Judge Wilson in Chattanooga issued an order for me to appear and start serving my sentence. I was to surrender myself on March 7 to the United States marshal at the Federal Building in Washington.

That's when I put Frank Fitzsimmons in the saddle, much to my later regret.

Going to prison isn't the kind of a day you forget. I told Jo and the kids that I didn't want them to go with me. It would have been just too much of an ordeal for them. You could bet that the whole Washington press corps would be there and it would have been as embarrassing as hell for my family.

I'm proud of my wife, Jo, and of my children. They never bowed their heads. They heard me called every conceivable name there was. They never bowed their heads. They knew one thing. To survive you must fight.

But by now, I figured, they had enough. I didn't want them to have to take any more.

Chuck O'Brien and Morris Shenker, my lawyer, were driving me down to the Federal Building. When we got into the car in the garage at our building, we just sat there for a few minutes without anybody saying anything.

"Well," I told them finally, "let's get going."

Chuck, as I said, had been with me for years and was almost like a son. At that time. He didn't want to start the car. He was all broke up.

Chuck was the son of a union organizer from the early days in Detroit. His mother, Sylvia, was a longtime friend of Jo's. They had walked picket lines together in the thirties. When Chuck was a child his father, Frank, died. We raised Chuck from the time he was six years old.

Now, as it came time for me to go away, he wasn't holding up as good as I was.

"We're not going anywhere," he said.

"C'mon," I told him. "What the hell, they can't eat me."

So off we went, and when we got close to the Federal Building there was a hell of a mob. There must have been two hundred newspaper, radio, and television guys waiting to see Jimmy Hoffa get the can tied to his tail.

"We can go around to the back door," Morrie suggested.

"Like hell," I said. "I never ran away from anybody and I'll be damned if I'm gonna start now. Drive this son of a bitch right up to the front door."

When we pulled up, and as I got out of the car, they started running toward us like a herd of wild elephants. Christ, I've seen smaller riots. It kind of reminded me of one of those movies where they throw the Christians to the lions.

One of the older reporters was trying to stay in the front. All of a sudden he tripped and fell down and I'll be damned if the guys in back didn't run right over him. All I could think of was that he was going to be hurt bad.

"Hold it! Hold it!" I yelled, waving my arms for them to back off. "For Christ's sake settle down."

I ran over and helped the old guy up and brushed him off.

Then—and I guess I'm a born organizer—I began getting those press guys in line.

"You TV guys over here on the right," I pointed. "You newspaper guys over here on the left. Okay, we'll start with the television guys first. I never ducked any of your questions before and I won't start now."

"How do you feel, Jimmy?" one guy hollered.

"I'm okay," I said. "And don't worry, I'll be back."

Then another one yelled: "Do you expect any special treatment in prison?"

"Yeah," I told him. "It'll be special, all right. My friend Robert Kennedy will see to that."

When the interviewing was over, we went up to the U.S. marshal's office. Everybody in the joint was running around like they were getting a screen test for the FBI show on television.

There still was one last-minute appeal pending before Judge Wilson. All I was trying to do was get time to finish negotiating a new contract for the nation's trucking industry before the old one ran out on March 31. What I was asking was a $600-million contract for the next three years. So I wanted to call and find out what was going on as far as a delay was concerned.

"I'd like to use a phone," I said, and you might have thought I'd asked for the key to Fort Knox. There was a lot more running around while they tried to decide whether it was all right for me to phone or whether Shenker would have to do it. Finally they said it was okay.

I picked up a phone and, honest to God, it fell apart right on the desk.

"You must have been bugged lately," I told them, laughing, "because it looks like somebody forgot and left a screw loose."

None of them laughed.

Then I used another phone and found out, as I'd expected, that Judge Wilson had denied our motion for a delay.

When I turned around, the head marshal was standing there.

"Okay," I told him, "let's get the hell out of here."

That's when they came with the chains and the shackles as if, for Christ's sake, I was John Dillinger, or somebody. Like I said, I don't know where the hell they thought I was gonna run to.

When we got down to their *Bonnie and Clyde* caravan,

the old newspaper guy I had helped up when the crowd was trampling him was standing there. And I'll be damned if he wasn't crying.

I got a card later from him when I was in prison. All he said was, "Thanks for caring."

It was quiet and I did a lot of thinking on that ride to Lewisburg. The hardest thing was leaving your family; not being able to see them anytime you wanted. Then I kept thinking about those days when the cops picked me up seven or eight times a day just for being on the picket line. They were just harassing me then. They knew it wasn't necessary and wouldn't do any good. It was the same with the chains these guys had put on me.

They weren't necessary either and they wouldn't really change anything.

I already had the key to my future in my head. I'd tough it out and whoever had a hard on for me in the future would have a hell of a time nailing me.

12

Convict

I hope you never have to go to prison. It's hell on earth, only hell couldn't be this bad.

I've listened to a lot of baloney for years about the preferential treatment I got in prison. Well, let me set you straight, it's all somebody's imagination or just plain damned lies.

The only preference I received was an arbitrary denial of my rights. When you go to prison they forget it's *your* Constitution, too.

When it was time for me to go they shackled and chained me like a wild animal: ten pounds of leg irons, belly band, handcuffs, and a chain running up from the leg irons to the handcuffs. There was a caravan to Lewisburg Federal Penitentiary that looked like a capture scene from *Bonnie and Clyde*. I don't know where the hell they thought I was going to run to.

Once we arrived and got inside, I did receive "preferential treatment." I was "processed" alone: booked, finger printed, stripped, run through a delousing shower, and shoved into isolation for twenty-four hours.

I don't care how tough you are; at a time like that you have to feel pretty hopeless and beaten. You think back over how you came to be there and only then, finally, did it strike me how much Bobby Kennedy had hated me: how for years he had spent millions of dollars of taxpayers' money and used every tool at the government's command to satisfy his own personal malice because of how I had manhandled him and kicked the hell out of his precious ego.

Guys have been known to hang themselves in isolation. But if you have guts you straighten your spine, stick out your jaw, and tell yourself they can all go to hell because you'll tough it out and you'll be back on the outside again just like before.

My case was a lot different than most of these guys inside Lewisburg. Sure, I had diabetes, but I had medication and aside from that I was strong and healthy. More important, waiting for me was a faithful family, financial security, and, hopefully, eventual return to my life work in unionism.

I didn't really get to thinking about those other guys inside until much later. Right then it was simply waiting to see what happened to Jimmy Hoffa. So I just kept my mouth shut when they ended my isolation period and marched me up to my cell. You want to know what it feels like to be buried alive? Well, my cell was seven and a half feet wide and ten feet long. My bunk bed was twenty-eight inches wide. There was a chair and a locker twenty-four by twelve inches. That left three and one-half feet to move around. Preferential treatment, right?

I spent fifty-eight months in Lewisburg and I can tell you this on a stack of Bibles: prisons are archaic, brutal, unregenerative, overcrowded hell holes where the inmates are treated like animals with absolutely not one humane thought given to what they are going to do once they are released. You're an animal in a cage and you're treated like one.

My first taste of it came right off the bat. When they put

me away I was a fringe diabetic and had to go to the doctor every two weeks. When I went in, I took along my medicine and a letter from one of the finest doctors in Georgetown Hospital explaining my condition. The first thing they did was tear up the letter and flush the pills down the toilet. Actually they did me a favor, the only one I can think of, because dieting and exercise cured me. No more diabetes.

Lewisburg was built in 1932 to accommodate 1050 prisoners. When I arrived it was jammed with 1800 people and on my first trip to the confined quarters of the exercise yard it seemed as if all of them knew me. There were all kinds: lifers, homosexuals, gunmen, forgers, burglars, safecrackers, you name it.

In all of them you could see the hope and the hopelessness; hope that they'd get sprung (paroled) and a hopelessness as to what they would do once they were on the outside again. And right there you have the major fault in our prison system.

License-plate and mop-bucket manufacturing are the two really big vocational training programs in prisons, and they have absolutely no relation to potential jobs in private industry for the ex-con. That is unless our goal is to train prisoners to go out and illegally manufacture and sell phony license plates for stolen cars.

They all had the same story. What were they going to do to make a living when they got back on the outside? Bitter, disturbed, and more antisocial and more skilled in crime than when they went in, the majority of them had little hope of going straight. God knows how many of them pleaded with me to see if I could find them a job. I began to feel like I was running an employment office.

Vicious guards, food you wouldn't feed to pigs, inadequate medical care, and easily obtainable dope made the joint a time bomb that was ready to explode at any moment.

There was plenty of dope and plenty of tranquilizers available. Three times a day they brought out the pill tray to keep everybody tractable. And you're damned right there was a black market for anything you wanted whether it was heroin, hashish, marijuana, or what have you. Bennies (Benzedrine) sold on the prison market for three dollars a pill. Black and reds (Dexedrine) were the same price. A dorie (Doriden) could be had for one dollar a pill, while red devils (Seconal) were five bucks and yellow jackets were six dollars per pill. And there was plenty of it, anything you wanted as long as you had money—or would sell your body.

How does the dope get in? Well, there are only two entrances. One is for trucks, and that's guarded carefully. The other is for visitors and guards. The visitors don't bring it in, for damned sure. So you figure it out.

And right here I'd like to say that any guy handling dope— whether he is an importer, a guy who cuts it, or a pusher— should be lined up against a wall and shot.

The guards in prison are something else, and I wasn't in there two weeks before I had my first run-in with one of the worst "hacks," the lowest term a con can call a guard. When I came back to my cell the door to my locker was open and he was sitting on my bunk reading my letters from home.

"What the hell do you think you're doing?" I asked him.

He looked up at me and sneered: "Just readin'."

"Put 'em back," I said, and he could see I was hot.

He dropped the letters on my bunk and stood up. "Don't try to get tough with me, Hoffa."

I damned near jumped him right there and if I had, the way I felt, I'd have busted him in half.

"Listen, hack," I said, trying to control my voice, "if I ever find you in my things again I'm going to make you the sorriest son of a bitch that ever set foot in this prison."

I meant it and he knew it. He walked out without another word.

There are three classes of prison guards. Eighty-five percent of them want the job because it gives them a pension and it's a better job than they can get on the outside because of their limited mentality and ability. All those kind want is to get along without trouble until they can collect their eventual pension.

If you think I'm running down their average mentality, you're right. One well-educated con who was in on a forgery rap wrote a letter in which he quoted Oscar Wilde. The guard in his cell block got hold of the letter and went to the con.

"What cell is this Oscar Wilde in?" he demanded, supposing that the prisoner was quoting another inmate.

Another prisoner who waited on the guards' mess told me of overhearing this conversation between two hacks:

"Say," the first guard observed, "how about that soup de jour?"

"What about it?" asked the other.

"Well," said the first, "they must have bought a hell of a lot of it because we been having it every day."

Humorous? Not at all. Illiterates placed in a position of power become dangerous. While I was at Lewisburg they held a written examination for guard candidates. Not a one passed the written test. Next they held an oral test. Nobody passed that one, either. So they just eliminated the test and made appointments at random.

Which brings us to the other 15 percent of the guards.

Two-thirds of those are eager beavers looking for promotion. To bring themselves to the attention of the front office they write up inmates for violations and all kinds of garbage.

Then there are the five percent who are plain sadistic bastards.

Their favorite targets were prisoners who were put into "the hole" for one reason or another. The hole is a cell ten by seven feet with a steel-covered window so that no light and little air gets in. It has a steel bunk fastened to the wall with chains and in the daytime they take away the mattress so you sit on the concrete floor or on the bare steel bunk. Prisoners are fed through an opening in a solid door and are permitted out only once a week to shower and shave.

At one time they had some Black Muslims in the hole and several guards would walk through every night and spray Mace into the cell through the food slot. The leader of the Muslims was a man about six feet four and 240 pounds and for no reason at all two guards squirted Mace into his face. When he came out of the hole he broke loose and damned near killed both of them before they could tear him away.

The main problem, as far as the guards are concerned, is that in Lewisburg—and it's true in every federal prison—there are no set rules that are standard. The guard details are rotated every ninety days and each guard applies his own set of rules to his cellblock. Maybe you'll have three good guards in a row who don't care if you have pictures on the wall or a stack of letters in your locker. Then a new guard comes in, one of the 5 percenters. He doesn't tell you to take down the pictures. He tears them down, rips them up, and throws the pieces on the floor. Then he takes your letters, reads them, and decides which ones and how many you can keep. He makes the decision. Which is why of all the trouble I saw in prison, 99 percent was created by the guards, not the inmates.

At one point a guard lieutenant drew up a set of sensible rules and distributed them to every cell. When the captain found out about it, he locked all the cellblocks until all the sets of rules were turned in and we went right back to the old system where individual guards could make their own rules in each cellblock.

But I'll tell you one thing. After my run-in with that one hack, nobody ever bothered *my* letters.

I have to admit, without blowing my own horn in any way, that I probably was something of a celebrity at Lewisburg. In some manner, truck drivers making deliveries to the prison— most of them Teamster members—found out where my cell was. Driving through the yard they'd lean out of their cabs and yell:

"Hiya, Jimmy, keep your chin up!"

"Hey, Jimmy baby, we're still with you!"

"Don't let 'em get you down, Jimmy!"

"If ya need anything, Jimmy, just let us know!"

The warden at one point called me into his office and asked me if I couldn't put a stop to such goings-on.

"Warden, what can I do?" I shrugged.

Nor could he do anything about it. The drivers weren't convicts who could be thrown into the hole. And I suggested with some tact that if he tried to get tough with them it just might be possible that the Teamsters would stop all deliveries to the prison.

He got the point.

On another occasion he summoned me to his office and said, "Listen, Hoffa, I want you to tell me something."

"What's that?" I asked him.

"I'd like you to tell me how it is that everybody who comes into this prison reports to you?"

"Well," I told him, "I didn't know that they did report to me. Who told you that?"

He frowned. "The guards have been telling me that no

matter who comes into this place, black, white, or brown, no matter who they are, they report to you. Why?"

I shook my head. "I didn't know they did that. But, assuming that it's so, what's wrong with it? I know a lot of people and they know me and I guess most of them just want to say hello."

"I'd like to know why they don't come to see me," he insisted.

Talking to him was better than being back working in the mattress factory, so I humored him. "I'd guess that maybe there are two reasons."

"What would they be?"

"Well, in the first place, they aren't learning a damned thing serving time here that will help them get a job and support themselves when they get sprung. A great many of them think I can help them get a decent job when they do get out."

"That makes sense," he said. "What else?"

I laid it on him. "The conditions in here are God-awful— bad guards, bad food, and bad everything. You're the man at the top and nothing is being done to make conditions better. Maybe they don't come to you because they don't respect you. Did you ever think of that?"

His face flushed red and he jumped to his feet. "That's enough of that! Out!"

The next day he had me taken back to his office.

"Sit down," he directed. "Have a cigarette."

"I don't smoke."

He didn't say anything for a couple of long minutes. "Jim," he said finally, "I've only got eighteen months to go to re- tirement and I haven't got a blemish on my record. Naturally, I don't want any trouble. Now, as I understand it, you could stop trouble or make trouble in this prison."

"Warden," I told him, "I don't know who told you that but it isn't true."

"All right, all right," he nodded. "You say it isn't true. But, as I told you, I've only got eighteen months to go and I don't want any trouble. So I'll ask you a favor. Anything that looks like it's going to cause trouble, you come and see me."

Not long after that the food started going from bad to worse. I told one of the guards that I wanted to see the warden but a couple of days went by and nothing happened.

Now you have to understand that Lewisburg had food delivered at the back door that was as good as any restaurant. A lot of it disappeared out that same back door. The rest was ruined by the system. The prison had a chief steward who was paid thirty-five thousand a year. He had fourteen stewards, each one supposed to be a chef. Most of those men were former guards who couldn't boil water. There were more than 150 working in the kitchen and most of them were cons sent there for punishment, like KP in the Army. The steward hacks made the cons do the cooking for the inmates. What comes out is unbelievable, usually cold, greasy, and on the verge of spoiling.

So on this particular day I decided to do something about it. I got myself at the head of the food line and they were about to ladle out some slop onto a dish when I see it bubbling. Not bubbling hot. Maggots.

"Hold it," I told the guy with the ladle, "I won't eat that garbage."

"Jimmy," whispered the con doling out the food, "take it easy or there'll be hell to pay."

"I ain't moving," I said in a loud voice, standing there with my arms folded and holding up the whole line.

Now one of the guards comes running over. "What's going on here? What's the trouble?"

"We're not going to eat this mess," I told him.

"What do you want to do, cause a riot?" he said and I mean he was really nervous.

"No," I told him quietly. "I want to see the warden."

"Christ," he muttered, and waved to a captain, who came over on the run.

"What the hell's going on?" the captain asked the guard.

"Hoffa," the guard pointed to me. "He says none of them are gonna eat this stuff and he says he wants to see the warden."

The captain tried to bluff it out. "C'mon, Hoffa, take the food and move along before you get into trouble."

I wasn't so quiet this time and the line behind me was getting restless and up tight. "You'll get trouble all right unless you get the warden down here and damned quick," I told him.

"Okay, okay, everybody take it easy," the captain almost shouted, turning and tearing out of the room.

It didn't take long for the warden to come running into the mess hall.

"Hoffa," he demanded, "what's going on here?"

"Take a look at that," I said to the warden, at the same time pointing at the food.

He looked at it and swallowed a couple of times like a man about to throw up.

"Well, we'll have to do something about that," he said and, turning to the guard captain, added, "Let's get something else in here right away."

All the guards and the kitchen help started scurrying around and the line just stood there.

"Hoffa," the warden said in a low voice after he pulled me aside, "I asked you to come to me if there was anything that might cause trouble. Why didn't you come and see me?"

"I tried to send word to you a couple of days ago but nothing happened," I told him. "How the hell can I come see you when you're locked away up there in your office? So the time came when something just had to be done and this was the only way I could see to do it."

He didn't want anything to do with any kind of trouble. "Hoffa, I'll tell you what I'm going to do. I'll agree that every day at twelve o'clock noon I'll walk in here and look over the food to determine whether it's all right."

"Will you eat it?" I asked him flat out.

"No."

"Then," I said, "you're just wasting your time."

"I'll do it anyhow," he volunteered.

Sure enough, every day at twelve o'clock sharp he'd open the steel grill, walk in and walk up and down. "Hello, boys. How are you? Blah, blah, blah."

Then he'd walk into the kitchen, look around, come out again, and inspect the food.

The food didn't improve a hell of a lot. But at least there were no more maggots.

I realize, of course, that a prison isn't supposed to be some kind of a country club. But, on the other hand, it shouldn't be allowed to deprive a man of his hope and his sanity. Yes, and even his health if he manages to stay alive. That last isn't too easy because there were four murders while I was at Lewisburg.

The first one I saw was in the so-called gymnasium, a place not half large enough for those who wanted to use it. One guy was working out on the punching bag when another con came up and said he wanted to use it.

"I'll be done in a couple of minutes," the fellow punching the bag said.

The other guy turned around and walked out. In a few minutes he came back, walked up behind the guy punching the bag, and stabbed him to death. The guy with the knife was already serving two life sentences. What do you give him, three?

But it tells you one thing. The difference between life and death in prison is the availability of weapons. Everybody has a knife because where there's metal there's a weapon. You have a metal bunk, you have a knife.

And you'd sure as hell better have a knife to protect yourself if you're between twenty-one and thirty because you're a prime target for rape. What do you expect when they throw young first offenders in with homosexuals and murderers? Most likely it's a gang rape, and it happens all the time. That was one of the main reasons John Dean didn't want to go in. So what happens to the guy who gets raped? He complains and they throw him into the hole and then ship him off to, say, Atlanta, where he can't see his family or his lawyer because it's too far for them to travel. So he's the victim and he's the one penalized. They have to keep those young guys separated from the hard cases.

I went to the warden and complained about one kid who was raped.

"Forget it," he told me. "Forget the rapes."

"What about the guys who did it?" I wanted to know.

"Hell," he threw up his hands, "what do you expect me to do? They're here for forty years anyhow."

Some of those who are homos don't want to be helped. They do it for "protection," for favors, for money to buy dope on the prison black market or because of a twisted mind. One such was the second man murdered while I was in Lewisburg. He was a homosexual who wanted to change "daddies." His former daddy cornered him in the boiler room and ran a knife through him.

We had one guy come in to Lewisburg who bragged that he had committed forty-seven rape jobs. He was a mean, nasty

148

son of a bitch and started throwing his weight around. Three of us got him alone in the yard.

"We got a friendly message for you," I told him. "You're not really as tough as you think you are. We got guys in here who could chew you up and spit you out and would be glad of the chance to do it. Personally I think they oughta take bastards like you and stand you up against a wall and shoot you. As far as most of us in here are concerned, you're expendable as hell. So if I was you I'd walk the chalk line and keep my mouth shut."

He got the message.

In 1968, after I'd been in Lewisburg a year, there was a riot and work stoppage because of intolerable conditions. I formed a committee to informally hear and act on complaints. I'd write memos to the warden, lodge protests, take up grievances, and get briefs filed. One kid came to me and told me the guard was going to take away his lawbooks. The lawbooks stayed. If they hadn't, there'd have been hell to pay.

All of this did help to improve conditions somewhat, but when you have twice as many men crammed into a prison designed for half their number it doesn't take much to spark a riot. An argument in a ball game exploded another riot in 1969, a free-for-all in which one of the men involved was stabbed to death.

The fourth murder was that of a stoolie whose information had sent a guy in my cellblock to Lewisburg for a forty-year stretch. Now he had been nailed himself and sent to Lewisburg. It was his death warrant. The guy he ratted on put a knife in him and the stoolie ran all the way to the prison hospital before dropping dead in the doorway.

Speaking of the prison hospital, there's another joke. There were two doctors for nearly two thousand people. One and a half, actually, because one doctor spent half of his time on paper work. But don't get sick after 4 P.M., because that's when the doctors go off duty.

If that happens, the guard decides for himself whether you're sick enough to go to the hospital and see what's known as an MTA (medical training assistant), who is neither pharmacist nor doctor but a civilian who can only dole out aspirin or wrap up a stabbing.

The "technicians" are another farce and God help you if you have a heart attack, particularly during the night. At best the "technician" who gives the X ray or the cardiogram is an inmate whose "training" consists of a book to read, a diagram, and four days' practice. When a "technician" graduates, he is given four days to "train" his replacement.

The food ruins your teeth and if you're in there more than a year you'll need expensive dental care when you come out. That's because they have another doctor and a half for dentistry. They don't fill teeth or make partials. Get a bad tooth and they yank it out. Case dismissed.

I started to have trouble with my teeth and I raised so much hell that they finally did give me some temporary fillings. Later, when I was taken out of prison for trial on charges of mismanaging the Teamster pension fund I got an order from the judge allowing me to go to a dentist every night when I left the courtroom to have my teeth filled properly.

It seems that even in prison I never could get away from courtrooms. While I was inside, a wave of prison-reform hearings started across the country. I was sitting in the mess hall when the warden came in with a group of congressmen who had come to look into conditions at Lewisburg. Congressman John Conyers spotted me and came over and shook hands.

"We want to find out how things are going here," he told

me. "I know they're going to try to give us the showboat tour
and I'm not interested in that. We want to talk to you alone
and then meet with the warden later."

"Great," I replied, and told him about our four-man
complaint committee which included a Puerto Rican, a black,
and a former Army major. "There are a lot of things that need
correcting."

Conyers nodded. "We've already been to several prisons
and have a good idea what's been happening. Suppose you
make up a list, Jim, and we'll go over them with you before
meeting with the warden."

I went back to my cell and wrote out a total of nineteen
complaints. Then I sent word to the congressmen that the committee was ready and we four were taken to a conference room
to meet with them.

First we went over my list and then one of our guys started
on a racial issue, how the guards discriminated against various
races. This was true enough, because those 5 percenters among
the guards took great delight in harassing blacks, Puerto
Ricans, Jews, and, in particular, anybody alleged to have
so-called Mafia connections. But I didn't feel that this was the
time for that.

"Hold it," I ordered. "Just a minute. We're not here to talk
about discrimination. We're here to try to get the prison
straightened out for everybody."

We discussed all angles of my nineteen complaints for
about two hours. Then the congressmen sent for the warden.

When he came into the room, the warden looked like an
advertisement out of one of those fashion magazines. He had
a passion for wearing matching outfits with everything in the
same color. This time he was all in green: shoes, socks, pants,
coat, tie, the works. He was a little bit of a guy who considered

himself the Napoleon of Lewisburg. And he wasn't about to let even a congressional committee tell him how to run the prison.

He sat down, folded his arms, and, looking at us four inmates, said, "I absolutely refuse to meet and discuss anything with the inmates before you gentlemen. Anything they might want is denied and any request they have will be denied. I'm the warden of this prison."

Conyers' eyes opened wide as if he couldn't believe his ears. "Now just a moment, Warden. This is a question of a congressional hearing. We are holding the hearing, not the inmates, and we want answers."

The warden stared right back at him. "I refuse to recognize your authority and I also refuse to answer any questions."

You could see Conyers was getting mad. "You're either stupid or something else is wrong with you and I'll tell you one thing for certain. You'll get a subpoena and you'll testify in front of our whole committee."

There was a newspaperman from the Milwaukee *Journal* with the congressmen and, when the warden just sat there with his arms folded and didn't answer, Conyers spoke up and asked me if he could have my list of complaints.

"You can't have them," the warden said. "It's against prison rules for Hoffa to have anything here in writing."

Conyers overrode him. "We'll make an exception in this case, warden. If Hoffa wants to give them to this man, he can do it."

"Here you are," I said, handing them over to the newspaperman.

The warden didn't know what to do so he just sat there and with the meeting at a dead end it broke up and the four of us on the inmates' complaint committee were taken back to our cells. About an hour later a guard came for me and took me back to the conference room where Conyers was waiting.

"Jimmy," he said, "I tried to reason with the warden and set up another meeting but he refused and told me he wouldn't discuss prison affairs with us. He claims there's nothing wrong with the prison and everything is all right here."

"Well, John," I told him, "I'll tell you what you do. Ask him if you can go to K Block, or over to C Block. Better yet, ask him if you can go to the hole."

"All right," Conyers agreed, and left. He was back in a few minutes looking grim. "He told me I couldn't see them."

I almost had to laugh. The warden had the brass to talk that way to a congressman but it wasn't news to me. What Conyers didn't realize was that every prison is like a ship with a captain. The warden answers to nobody. Usually he comes up through the ranks from guard to warden, a key in the left hand and a club in the right, and he exercises total control.

"That's the way it is," I shrugged.

"Like hell it is," Conyers exploded. "We'll settle that gentleman's hash with a subpoena to appear in Washington."

Conyers was as good as his word.

Not long afterward I was told that I would be taken to Washington the following day to appear before the congressional committee on prison reform. The warden must have blamed me for most of his troubles, having been subpoenaed, too.

That night he clapped me in the hole.

Outside of being in solitary overnight in a completely blacked-out room it wasn't too bad. Most guys thrown in the hole were stripped bare. They gave me my outside clothes and, it being nighttime, I also had a mattress of sorts for that steel bunk.

153

When I was taken to Washington, I told my lawyer about it. He was furious and obtained a court order restraining prison authorities from ever putting me in the hole if and when I was to be taken outside again for any reason.

Nothing of any consequence happened at the congressional hearing on prison reform. I testified as to the miserable conditions, but mostly it was water off a duck's back. Hell, it's always the same. Like you make a guy a judge or a district attorney, hoping he's humane, and he becomes a bastard. They start off right and when they start seeing too many crooks and too much lowlife they get so they throw them in jail to forget them. He says, "The class of people I see! The dirt that comes in front of me!" So why don't they quit? Not them. They're thinking of the pension.

So I felt that all I was doing before the committee was spinning my wheels. But I did tell them that the deplorable conditions in prison had accounted for four murders just since I had been there.

"That's not true," the warden protested.

"What's not true?" he was asked.

"There have been only three murders," he said.

Christ!

The hearing ended up like some kind of a comedy.

The warden read a prepared statement from the Bureau of Prisons. It painted such a beautiful picture that, when he was finished, one of the congressmen said:

"Warden, hearing this, I'd like to know whether I could make a reservation for my wife and my children to spend a vacation at your prison, it sounds so nice."

Everybody broke up laughing.

But I can tell you this: our prisons and their conditions are no laughing matter.

13
Outside Again

There are no special "tough guys" in prison. Everybody's tough. You have to be if you're going to survive those first ninety days. That's when your guts are tested and if you aren't tough enough you'll wind up in a mental hospital.

It takes those three months to get over the feeling that the world has ended. Everything's strange, strange and hard. I don't give a damn who you are, they try to give you a certain amount of hassle. The other cons test you, and the guards, in particular, try to give it to you because they want you to know they're the bosses. If you let them, they'll roust the hell out of you. So you have to let them know that you're not going to be a wise guy or a troublemaker but by God you're not going to take a lot of crap, either.

I went through it although, I have to admit, maybe not as much of it as some of them have to take. Everybody knew that I'd been through the mill ever since I was a kid. And, while I was fifty-four years old when I went in, I was in damned good physical condition and I guess nobody had to be told that I could take care of myself.

Nobody will ever know how much I missed Jo and the kids most of all. That was probably the worst of it because

I've always been a family man first and everything else came second. The rest of the crap they dished out I could handle. But you never get over counting the days even after you settle into the monotonous prison routine.

One thing that really bothered the hell out of me all the time I was in the joint was the bright light they kept on right outside the cell door. Then in the middle of the night, when you finally did manage to fall asleep, they'd come in and shine a flashlight in your face to make sure you were still there. With all those steel doors, I wondered where the hell they thought I'd be going.

I'd been in Lewisburg one year and four months when Robert Kennedy was shot in June of 1968 in San Francisco. I can't honestly say that I felt bad about it. Our vendetta had been too long and too strong. Over the years I'd come to hate him and yet when he got it I felt nothing. But don't think I was the only one who had hated him. I want it known that a hell of a lot of people felt the same way I did about him.

I'm not being vindictive against a guy who's dead, but I have a newspaper clipping which kind of proves what I've been saying about him all along. It's a story written by Robert S. Boyd, chief of the Knight Newspapers' Washington bureau, and it appeared on Thursday, June 6, 1968, right after he'd been shot while celebrating his victory in the California presidential primary. It says:

> If Robert Kennedy had made it to the White House, his presidency could have been destroyed by the same hate that drove a bullet into his brain Wednesday.
>
> Rarely has a public figure been the object of such widespread, passionate loathing as the boyish-looking senator from New York. . . .
>
> The anti-Kennedy fever was not confined to any

one group or section of the nation, though perhaps it raged more virulently in the South and the West.

Traveling correspondents found the same emotion scattered from Maine to California. A group of dentists in New England expressed almost unbelievable animosity toward Kennedy at a convention there last weekend.

At a Republican rally in Charlotte, N.C., the mere mention of Kennedy's name last month set off boos and a frenzied chant of "Hippie, hippie, hippie."

A liberal New York Democrat, now retired in Florida, talking politics a few hours before the shooting, declared angrily: "The one person I couldn't stand to see in the White House is that demagogue Bobby Kennedy." . . .

The resentment seems to stem more from what many considered his excessive ambition—he was portrayed as a greedy rich kid grabbing for a prize he wouldn't deserve if he weren't Jack Kennedy's little brother.

Some statements by Kennedy indicating that he valued his personal career above the welfare of his party and country added to this impression. . . .

Although the senator tried hard to live down his "ruthless" reputation, some of his aides and associates, in their zeal, struck outsiders as rude, arrogant and pushy.

And, in this connection, I have to give you one more clincher. A letter since has come to light, written by Dwight D. Eisenhower on March 26 of that year, in which the former president said he found Kennedy "shallow, vain and untrustworthy." The letter added, "It is difficult for me to see a single qualification that the man has for the presidency."

If you think I pass those along with satisfaction, you're right.

In November of 1969, at the end of the year following Robert Kennedy's assassination, I became eligible for parole. It was denied without any reason ever being given and I wasn't eligible to apply for parole again until March 31, 1971.

On March 27, 1971, four days before that parole review date rolled around, there was a significant break in my case.

Edward Grady Partin, the stool pigeon whose perjury sent me to prison at Chattanooga, had become involved as I understand it in some sort of a business deal with Audie Murphy. The movie star, who had been America's most decorated hero of World War II, was said to want a favor from me, although I never found out what it was. He was subsequently killed in that mysterious plane crash. Anyhow, Murphy thought it would put him in with me, I guess, because through his efforts and those of attorney Irving Kramer there was a breakthrough.

Partin made a deposition in Sherman Oaks, California, which spelled out in detail under Kramer's questioning how I had been railroaded.

Senator George Murphy personally took it to Attorney General John Mitchell and Audie Murphy gave it to President Nixon.

It was a twenty-nine-page confession and it is so important in my eyes that, while it is too long to be given in full, I will quote the vital points that prove how Robert Kennedy's Get-Hoffa Squad managed to obtain their dirty, rigged conviction. Remember that this is the affidavit under oath of Edward Grady Partin, the man whose perjured testimony convicted me at Chattanooga and sent me to prison unjustly for nearly five years.

His first admission was that he was coached and told what to say every day of the trial by government attorneys.

Partin next admitted that Judge William Daniels of Baton Rouge taped his three calls to me.

QUESTION: He [Hoffa] didn't know this was being recorded?
ANSWER: No.

And:

QUESTION: Did he call you or did you call him?
ANSWER: I called him.

And:

QUESTION: When you called him what did you say?
ANSWER: They had written down the questions for me to ask him.

The second time, too, when he called me, he said, they told him what to ask me particularly about what was to be the basis of my defense. On the third call, Partin deposed, "They wanted me, in effect, to get in his camp and find out what was going on" and they had put up his bond. Then this was his reply when asked what happened on his arrival in Nashville.

ANSWER: I had been in Mr. Hoffa's suite of rooms and I met Mr. Grimsley [of the Justice Department staff] around the corner from the Andrew Jackson Hotel and they wanted to know what was going on during the course of Hoffa's conference with the attorneys.

Partin said that these meetings with Grimsley were held daily and under instructions he reported everything he overheard in our conferences. He also said he did it because he was threatened with "a life sentence for kidnapping" and "a chance of the electric chair."

"They had everything sewed up," he said. "They had the Attorney General [RFK]. They had the President [JFK]. They had the district attorney where I lived, so I don't think you can get any more stronger than that as far as having to do what they said to do."

Partin denied in the affidavit that I had ever offered him any money or said I would offer money for jury fixing, as he had testified at Chattanooga. He said that the "ten or twenty thousand" I mentioned was what my legal defense was costing, but the government agents said, "No, that wasn't what he [Hoffa] meant. He [Hoffa] was talking about potential jury people."

And, he added, they were "calling the Attorney General every day and telling the progress of the case." Meaning Robert Kennedy, of course.

If you don't believe we were bugged and our phones were tapped, in addition to Partin's daily reports to the FBI, consider this statement he made in the affidavit:

> It seemed to me that they knew what Hoffa was going to do, because the questions that would be given [to me], would be to counteract what they [Hoffa's attorneys] put on the next day, and *they would fit in perfectly*.

Remember that Partin made this affidavit on March 27, 1971.

He was asked if, after the Chattanooga trial, there was someone from the FBI with him "all the time."

"Until," he said, "approximately eighteen months ago."

Meaning until September of 1968.

One and a half years after I had gone to prison!

And until three months after Robert Kennedy was shot!

QUESTION: Until long after the trial?

ANSWER: *Long* after the trial. . . . They ran them in teams. They [agents] would stay two weeks at a time and come back two weeks at a time and I knew then there had to be something wrong or they wouldn't be guarding me.

Four days after Partin gave that affidavit, on March 31, 1971, my second appeal for parole was denied even though my wife, Jo, was in critical condition with a heart ailment. The word came down to us that the parole was denied because I had kept my union ties.

So, on June 22, 1971, I resigned as general president of the Teamsters in favor of Frank Fitzsimmons, sending this advisory to the Teamster executive board meeting in Miami. Fitzsimmons already had made his move.

Because I find it highly significant that a short time later —on that very same day—President Nixon went to that executive board meeting in Miami to congratulate Fitzsimmons on becoming general president of the Teamsters.

Then, two days later so that they would have no more excuses to refuse my parole, I resigned my last Teamster position, as president of Local 299 in Detroit. Maybe that was the hardest job of all; I had been head for so long of that local, which was my starting place so many, many years earlier.

On August 20, 1971, my son, Jimmy, made a third appeal to the parole board and again it was denied. The word was that the board was "not convinced that Hoffa has severed all his ties with the union."

It was a stall. During all this time that my appeals were being batted back and forth, Fitzsimmons was living high on the hog and was being romanced by Nixon and his White House aides. The eventual Watergate bunch wanted Teamster support for Nixon in the 1972 election. That's where Dean came into collusion with Colson, who wanted that juicy Teamster law contract for his firm, and with Fitzsimmons. They were plotting to have the conditions put on my parole so that Fitzsimmons could keep the job.

When Fitzsimmons says he didn't know about the conditions that I couldn't participate in union activities until 1980, he's a liar. For Colson said publicly, "I advised Mr. Fitzsimmons I think the day before Hoffa was to be released that he was going to be released under conditions." All of that's a lot of crap because they'd planned it for a long time.

It came out right in the open on Jim Kincaid's ABC News *Close-up* program in November of 1974. On that show, William Carlos Moore, former head of DRIVE, the Teamsters' political arm, said he heard Fitzsimmons on the phone with Colson planning the restriction.

Moore said: "So he picked up his phone and asked his secretary to get Mr. Colson on the phone and he called Mr. Colson 'Chuck.'"

In a signed affidavit to the U.S. District Court, Moore deposed that Fitzsimmons said: "Chuck, Hoffa should be released from prison but I think it awfully important that a condition be placed on him that he not be free to seek office and to participate in the labor movement until after he has served his full sentence."

Moore added, on the TV program, "It became a kind of a standing rule with the administration—I'm talking about the Fitzsimmons administration—that let's get Hoffa out of jail, let's get the Hoffa people off our back, but let's restrict him so he cannot come back into the labor movement."

Dean set it up to ensure Fitzsimmons' support for Nixon and Colson's payoff was that when he left the White House for private practice his firm was hired immediately by Fitzsimmons to represent the Teamsters. Dean said he originated the restriction with Attorney General John Mitchell's approval. But that's a goddamned lie, too, as I'll prove right here.

Those conditions barring me from union activity until 1980 were not listed in the normal "Conditions of Parole" form which I signed on December 22, 1971. That form lists only the usual conditions: that the parolee shall not violate any law, drink to excess, use drugs, or have firearms. They tried to say later that the warden told me. Another damned lie. He didn't.

I signed that form in prison on December 22.

Nixon's commutation document with the conditions was signed by him on December 23.

Like I said, if I'd known of those conditions I wouldn't have accepted the commutation. Hell, I'd have been out without any restrictions in 1974.

And I didn't learn about them until I got to the Williamsport airport and was told by a reporter.

It was the first time in history that a president of the United States imposed a condition on the commutation of a sentence· with respect to a man's livelihood. It was a rigged violation of the double-jeopardy clause. It was a violation of the right of free association under the First Amendment as well as the right to earn a livelihood under the Fifth Amendment.

Watergate proved what that whole bunch was capable of doing and Dean, who ratted on everybody to get a deferred sentence and go free without bond, lied like hell when he said Mitchell approved those conditions on my commutation.

For in my continuing fight to have those restrictions lifted—a fight I'm going to win—I obtained two affidavits from John Mitchell throwing the lie in Dean's teeth.

The first affidavit from Mitchell, taken on October 15, 1973, deposes:

1. That neither I, as Attorney General of the United States, nor, to my knowledge, any other official of the Department of Justice during my tenure as Attorney General, initiated or suggested the inclusion of restric-

tions in the Presidential commutation of James R. Hoffa.

2. That President Richard M. Nixon did not initiate with or suggest to me nor, to my knowledge, did he initiate with or suggest to any other official of the Department of Justice during my tenure as Attorney General that restrictions on Mr. Hoffa's activities in the labor movement be a part of any Presidential commutation for Mr. Hoffa.

Dean contended that he had, subsequent to the Attorney General's disapproval of conditions, again discussed those conditions with Mitchell and they had been approved.

Mitchell denied Deans' "alleged conversations" in another affidavit on June 11, 1974.

> For Mr. Dean did tell me in December, 1971, that a condition disqualifying Mr. Hoffa from trade union management in the Warrant of Executive Clemency was under consideration. I immediately raised the question as to the legality of such a condition. I told Mr. Dean to take up the matter of legality of such a condition in the Warrant with Mr. Lawrence Traylor, the Pardon Attorney in the Department of Justice. I do not recall ever receiving a memorandum on the legality of the insertion of a condition in the Warrant from Mr. Dean or Mr. Traylor. I did not authorize Mr. Dean, Mr. Traylor or anyone else to insert such a condition in the Warrant. My discussions with Mr. Dean did not relate to the desirability or propriety of the inclusion of such a condition. They related solely to the question of its legality.

> At no time ever in the conversation with Mr. Dean or otherwise did I give any consideration to the necessity or desirability of the inclusion of a condition.

> I never revised, modified or amended the recommendation of the commutation of Mr. Hoffa's sentence which I made to the President in my letter of advice.

By this time I was ready to fight the whole world and we filed suit in the U.S. District Court in Washington in 1974 against President Nixon on the grounds that the conditions he signed, knowingly or not, had been done for "impermissible and illegal purposes." We named then Attorney General William B. Saxbe as a co-defendant and declared that the conditions were an illegal ax over my head.

So the fight goes on, and will go on as long as I have a breath left in my body.

I have been asked many times why I want to come back as general president of the Teamsters; why not sit back and take it easy?

I would give up everything I have except my family to run the Teamsters again. For running the Teamsters is like directing the largest corporation in America. I worked at it six and even seven days a week. Today we have a social president and a social secretary-treasurer who are out golfing and shaking hands with those who like the notoriety. They're not doing a job. I'm just afraid that if something isn't done this union is going to be in great trouble.

That's one reason. There are two others.

First of all, I've put forty-seven years of my life into the Teamsters. It's my whole life's work and you don't just throw that away when you're still healthy and strong enough to keep getting the job done.

The second reason is that I see one last big round of fights coming between labor and management. I've said consistently that no employer ever really accepts a union. They tolerate the unions. The very minute they can get a pool of unemployment they'll challenge the unions and try to get back what they call management's prerogatives, meaning hire, fire, pay what you want. I've been saying that ever since I came out of prison.

I'm convinced this war is going to take place and I want to be a part of it. In the old days they bombed our homes, shot us, used tear gas on us, and beat the hell out of us. It can happen the first time there's a depression and there would be a knockdown, bloody battle again. And when it's over the unions will be a bigger part of this government than ever before.

When that war comes, Jimmy Hoffa wants to be right up front.

And, as I said in the beginning, you can bet on it because I'll be back.

14

The National Association for Justice

Ed Lawrenson is a guy who had the same kind of vendetta with J. Edgar Hoover that I had with Robert Kennedy. The only thing is that the frame against Lawrenson cost him twelve and a half years in prison.

Big Ed was a mortgage broker in Phoenix when he made a business trip to Washington. While he was there he met a girl and invited her to visit Miami with him. When they were getting ready to leave, she asked Lawrenson if he would loan his automobile to her stepson while they were gone.

Ed was enjoying himself at the Fountainbleu Hotel in Miami Beach when he was arrested.

The stepson, one Robert Cutler, and a friend named Robert Couch had used Ed's car to rob a bank at Mechanicsville, Maryland, in a $29,000 heist. They ditched Lawrenson's car at the scene.

Arrested in Miami Beach, Ed was bug-eyed when he was charged, not with conspiracy, but with bank robbery. Cutler, who had borrowed his car, signed an affidavit that Lawrenson knew nothing about the pair's plan to hold up the bank. But at a subsequent hearing Cutler copped the Fifth and Lawrenson was hooked. He even had to pay back the $29,000, which was adding a hell of a lot of insult to illegal injury.

After a long trial, and an FBI supported decision which Lawrenson appealed all the way to the Supreme Court, Big Ed was sentenced to Atlanta Federal Penitentiary. Twelve and a half years is a damned long time for something you didn't do and Lawrenson had plenty of time to think. An educated man, he became a "jailhouse lawyer" who decided that when he did get out he was going to do everything he could to help prison inmates and ex-cons. As a start, while he was inside he devised and prepared the corporate work for an organization which he started upon his release.

This is the National Association for Justice, which he founded in 1972 and which is pledged to improving the conditions of those on the inside and in assisting inmates once they are released.

The co-founder of NAJ, Lillian B. Goldstein, a prominent Washington restaurant owner, who has worked with ex-offenders for 15 years, became NAJ's national president. Lil, now Mrs. Ed Lawrenson, is a person who calls it the way it is. Ben Weintraub, while a student at American University, was selected to head up the office staff. Ben is destined to be one of the nation's leading attorneys upon completion of his education. When mutual friends introduced us, I knew right off they were for real.

And, as a guy who only too damned well understood the lousy conditions in our prisons, I was intrigued by their ambitious plans and their astounding figures that there are 500,-000 prisoners in this country and each one costs the taxpayers at least ten grand a year.

It's ridiculous that neither the taxpayer nor the prisoner is getting his money's worth.

I knew first hand that our correctional system wasn't doing the job. But I was shook up to learn that more than seventy percent of the crimes in this nation are committed by former convicts. Why? Just because there is little, if any, "rehabilitation" in prison. I knew that helping cons was a joke and that prisons create hardened criminals.

So I jumped at the chance to help Big Ed, Lil, Ben, and the staff when, in April of 1973, Lawrenson offered me the post as director of the NAJ's Crisis Control Center. It was a helluva challenge. NAJ has an open telephone line 24 hours a day and as director of the Crisis Control Center I had to stay ready at any hour of the day or night to grab a plane with Ed and jump to any prison in the country to offer our help in mediating disputes or putting the clamps on a riot. And we have answered hundreds of calls for help.

People who would like to get my scalp say that I was working with the NAJ because it helped me get around all over the country and under the pretext of helping prisoners I was able to keep in personal touch with Teamster officials and build up support for the time I'd run for re-election as General President. That's a lot of bunk. I don't need to build up any support. It's there, just waiting for the time to back me. They know that Hoffa is their man and doesn't belong to either the Washington big shots or the mobsters.

I honestly believe in what the NAJ is doing and you can bet that when I'm back in office the Teamsters will get behind this movement. There was another reason why I joined in the NAJ program.

The prisoners will listen to somebody who's been there, like me or Big Ed. They know we mean what we say.

And remember this: riots are caused by prisons. That's because they treat the inmates like wild animals. Prisoners get to the point where they don't give a good goddamn whether they win or lose; they only want to prove that they should be treated as if they were men and not caged beasts.

It's about time we faced the fact that our prison system is a monumental screw-up. The federal government and many state governments have spent billions trying to clean up our cities and have spent peanuts to modernize and upgrade our prisons. Get a load of this:

• The U.S. Penitentiary at McNeil Island in the state of Washington was opened in 1889. Franklin D. Roosevelt was seven years old. It was built for 1000. It has nearly 1500 prisoners.

• The U.S. Penitentiary at Leavenworth, Kansas, was opened in 1895. Dwight D. Eisenhower was five years old. It was built for 1000. It has almost 2500 prisoners.

• The U.S. Penitentiary in Springfield, Illinois, was opened in 1902. Lyndon B. Johnson was six years old. It was built for 1000. It has 2200 prisoners.

• The Lewisburg, Pennsylvania, Penitentiary was opened in 1932. Jimmy Hoffa was nineteen years old. It was built for 1000. It has almost double that number.

• As late as 1940, the U.S. Penitentiary at Terre Haute, Indiana, was opened. That was more than a year before Pearl Harbor. It was built for 1000. It was nearly 1500 prisoners.

Which means that under overcrowded conditions and brutal treatment it's damned small wonder that all hell breaks loose in our prisons from time to time, and maybe not often enough or something might be done. In this country of ours we are spending a hell of a lot of money to perpetuate an archaic prison system. Consider this: Of our nation's cash layout for so-called corrections, 95 percent goes for custody, meaning steel doors. stone walls, and guards.

Only 5 percent is spent on health services, education, and rehabilitative employment training.

That's a hell of a way to run a railroad.

I had set up a grievance committee in Lewisburg and we were able to do a lot of good. I also helped guys get jobs on the outside. I know from personal experience that two of the major problems are that on the inside the inmates don't learn anything that will be useful on the outside and when they do come out they're branded as ex-cons and nobody wants to give them a chance to make an honest living. So we have a ridiculous rate of recidivism.

Like I said earlier, they teach you to make license plates and mop buckets. When an offender has done his time he is cut loose without having been helped. Now what the hell do they think he's going to do for a living? You think he's going to sit down somewhere and starve? Eighty-five percent of those leaving prison don't have a marketable skill, so it's no wonder they wind up back in the joint again.

And take a look at those prisons which do teach "useful" skills. Former judge Samuel Leibowitz said it all when he told about busted-down manual typewriters used to teach typing in an age of electric machines "and shoemaking equipment that even the little elves don't use anymore."

The National Association for Justice has a twenty-seven-point program, but right here I'll give you ten that I consider the most important.

1. Prison health services need to be improved and inmates should not be made to do paramedical work without proper training. There should be a qualified medical staff on duty twenty-four hours a day, not like at Lewisburg, where the

two doctors worked banking hours and nearly two thousand men could settle for aspirin the rest of the time.

2. Guards should receive formal training in penology with salaries that would attract the right kind of men and get rid of the sadistic "hacks" that cause a great deal of the trouble in prisons.

3. Food should be equivalent to cafeteria-style food on the outside. The garbage they throw at inmates contributes to anger and resentment that leads to riots, as I well know. Prisoners should be allowed to spend two bucks a day in a well-stocked commissary. The thirty-five dollars a month they're allowed just about pays for coffee and cigarettes.

4. This is one you might expect from a union man, but you can't imagine how it would help. Prisoners should be paid decent wages for their work. Leaving prison with thirty-five dollars in your pocket is using slave labor and setting a guy loose to go out and get money any way he can.

5. The system must train inmates for productive work and help them find jobs on the outside.

6. They have to separate the hard-core criminals from the first offenders. What the hell do they expect is going to happen when they put young guys in with hardened degenerates? I'll tell you: rape, violence, and the young guy who made one slip becomes a menace to society.

7. Better recreational facilities and adequately stocked libraries are essential.

8. A furlough program should be implemented at all prisons, which it hasn't been. This has been approved by Congress, granting four incentive furloughs a year for inmates who have not had a disciplinary report in the past year. Only a very few wardens are using it. Why? It's too damned much trouble. So they lock 'em up and throw the key away.

9. Advise prisoners why their parole has been refused. As it is now, the prisoner eligible for parole is at the mercy of the parole board. If the inmate has a good record and is turned down, he has no way of knowing why he was refused. That damned well needs changing. I was up for parole three times and twice there was absolutely no reason given as to why I was denied.

10. There should be more caseworkers assigned to prisons. They don't get the job done because they have too many prisoners to work with.

The biggest problem we've had is in dealing with prison authorities. They say they aren't going to "coddle" criminals. That's a lot of crap. They're just drunk with their own power. Wardens are the bosses, accountable to nobody. They're the captain of the ship and they damned well want everybody to know it. Most of them are looking for the pension and don't want trouble. Which proves how stupid they are. If they tried to be more humane they'd make the prisoners less hostile and there'd be less trouble.

I'll give you two cases of how we are resisted, even though all we want to do is help.

We got word that a damned dangerous situation was developing at Joliet, in Illinois. We requested permission to enter the prison, find out what was causing the unrest, and try to calm things down.

Our request was denied.

Shortly afterward there was a bloody riot at Joliet that caused two hundred thousand dollars' worth of damage.

We constantly get reports of explosive conditions shaping up at various institutions. One developed at Lucasville, Ohio, where a series of incidents caused the warden to take severe disciplinary action.

The inmates were kept naked and fed only cold meals for an entire week.

The joint was about to bust wide open. We were refused admission to the prison so we went to Governor John Gilligan. As a result of our conference, conditions at the prison were changed. The prisoners were clothed and fed properly and the situation at Lucasville cooled off.

It's one of our purposes to see that there are no more Joliets or Atticas. And where our cooperation was accepted we've gotten the job done. We settled things down at Lorton Reformatory in Lorton, Virginia; resolved a strike and riot at the Washington, D.C., jail, and averted riots at the Detention Center in Rockville, Maryland, and at the Baltimore city jail.

It's been a slow haul but we're making progress. The District of Columbia's Office of Personnel revised its policy of hiring ex-offenders. Now former inmates can be hired on any job they're qualified for as long as it isn't related to a crime for which they were convicted. We got a ton of letters from guys inside when in April of 1974 the Supreme Court tossed out prison rules which gave guards the right to hold back any mail they deemed "inappropriate." Letters from home mean a hell of a lot to a guy who's locked away from the rest of the world. Believe me, I know. And some son of a bitch who had a hard on for you could tear up your mail just out of goddamned meanness.

A lot of government officials stuck their noses up in the air when Ed Lawrenson started this thing. They figured, what the hell, this was a beef being fronted by a bunch of ex-cons. Getting acceptance was slower than a big rig fighting its way up Pike's Peak. But they're coming around.

We don't say that all prisoners should be set free. And we haven't been on the side of prisoners in disputes if we found out that their beefs were phony. But there is so damned much wrong with prisons, their administration and the system in general that there's a hell of a lot of work ahead of us.

But now it's finally starting to roll like a diesel going downhill and a lot of people can take credit for helping. Redd Foxx, the comedian, is our national chairman and actress Betsy Palmer is our national co-chairman. Melvin Belli, the noted San Francisco attorney, is special counsel to NAJ. We've also had a lot of help from people like singers Tony Martin and Johnny Desmond, comic Marty Allen, television stars Mike Douglas, Gail Fisher and Tige Andrews, and toastmaster general Joey Adams.

A bunch of important congressmen and senators are helping, too. They include men like Senators Charles Percy and Edward Brooke of Massachusetts, John Conyers of Michigan, William Lehman and Dante Fascell of Florida, Parren Mitchell of Maryland, and Congressmen Hamilton Fish, Jr., Mario Biaggi and former Congressman Ken Gray.

And let me say right here that anybody can belong to NAJ.

You can bet that I'm going to still maintain my position as director of NAJ Crisis Control Center, even after the Teamsters again take priority over everything but my family.

National Association for Justice Headquarters, 1100 17th Street, N.W., Washington, D.C. 20036. Hotline: 800–424–8625.

Bumper Sticker

An Epilogue by Oscar Fraley

Jimmy Hoffa's work with the NAJ possibly was to be the final chapter of his book as he awaited a court decision on the appeal to have those restrictions lifted from his commutation.

"But," he said, "we'll have a hell of a last chapter if things break as quick as I expect."

When we first met at his tenth-floor apartment in the Blair House at Miami Beach the appeal was foremost in his mind. Yet he talked of many things, then and in subsequent taping sessions.

His mind was sharp and his memory amazingly retentive as to dates, names, and places. An avid reader, he spoke knowledgeably and with deep conviction on a variety of subjects including economics, finances, politics and:

Dope peddlers and rapists: "Put 'em up against a wall and shoot the sons a bitches." Busing: "Go to school in your own neighborhood no matter who lives there." Capital punishment: "Damned right." Fear in the cities: "Crack down on the hoodlums; shoot their asses off." Gun control: "Without legal guns it'd be even worse. We gotta stop the shooters, not the guns." Welfare: "Sure take care of the old. But in Detroit there are families been on welfare three straight generations and they never look for a job. You give a bum a buck every day and the first day you miss he'll say, 'Where's my buck, you son of a bitch?'" The economy: "It's going to hell in a hand-basket."

At that very first meeting he handed me a batch of newspaper clippings and a pile of books. Most of it had to do with Robert F. Kennedy.

"Read this stuff," he commanded. "And use it. I want everybody to know I wasn't the only one who thought Robert Kennedy was a son of a bitch."

Kennedy and Frank Fitzsimmons were constantly recurring topics, quite naturally, and when the question arose as to why Fitzsimmons would even want him out of jail he thundered: "My people were raising hell and he wanted to quiet them down. Getting me out—with conditions—worked two ways for him."

Even in the relaxed atmosphere of his own living room, Hoffa sat ramrod-straight as if to compensate for his short stature. Seeming almost as broad as he was tall, he was a muscularly solid figure; a concrete Buddha with a brush haircut. For at sixty-two he did pushups daily and worked with weights three times a week.

Jimmy Hoffa remembered that as a young man he dreaded speaking in public. But you can ignore those who would have you believe that he had become a vocal wanderer. Hoffa was a spellbinder, the deep, positive voice rapping out its words with sledge-hammer decisiveness.

There was about him a magnetic quality and he talked of the power struggle ahead with an almost joyful anticipation. Combat had, after all, been his way of life. And his faith never wavered that "my guys," the nation's truckers who are the backbone of the Teamsters, would stand behind him in a showdown.

You had to believe him. As one old-line trucking company owner told me: "To the Teamsters, Jimmy was God. They knew he was always fighting for them, physically if necessary.

And I'll tell you another thing. He word was as good as gold; a handshake was better than a bale of legal papers drawn up by a battery of lawyers."

He laughed when I told him that, a deep rumble coming out of the broad chest like the sound of a subway train. "You see? They all knew I was the boss."

It launched him into his warlike charges against those he accused of bilking him out of the Teamster leadership, a firecracker recitation of frauds, kickbacks, and complicity with the underworld. Point by point, he ticked them off on thick, square fingers that could double into fists like mauls. And there would be more, "many more," he said, when he got those hands on the Teamster pension-fund books.

"Don't you worry that someone might try to do something to you?" I asked, pointing out that he was challenging men who were utterly merciless.

The green-blue eyes crackled. "I've never been one damned bit concerned about my safety. Nobody's going to bother me. After all, I took care of myself all my life."

Big Ed Lawrenson, head of the NAJ, asked him at one point what he would do if someone ever kidnapped a member of his family. For this was a man who put his family above everything in the world.

Hoffa's eyes turned slate-hard and the voice rasped. "Very simple. I'd have a press conference and I'd put up a million dollars cash for the head of the kidnapper. The case would be solved in forty-eight hours and I'd have the kidnapper's head."

I began having tape-recorder trouble toward the end of our interviews. "The hell with it," he said. "You can remember what I'm telling you. I never keep no notes, no letters. I remember everything I want to know."

We finished up, except for minor questions that I could ask him later on the telephone, and he got ready to "take the family up to the lake." That was his four-acre summer home at Lake Orion, forty miles north of Detroit, where his son, young Jim, has a home nearby.

After several telephone conversations, we both flew to New York for a June 25 meeting with publisher Sol Stein, Jimmy coming in from Detroit. For two hours over lunch, Hoffa kept the conversational bit in his teeth, enthralling a group which included Lawrenson, editor George Caldwell, and literary agents Anita Diamant and Ruth Hagy Brod. He was on stage and he loved it.

When we were riding back to the airport, he looked at me with a big grin and said: "How'd I do?"

"Jimmy," I told him, "you're beautiful."

He roared with laughter, slapping my knee with one meaty hand. "Hardly that." He laughed again, head thrown back.

"I'll see you later," he said, bouncing out of the car at his air terminal, eager to get back to Jo and the family. "Take care!"

There were more phone calls, getting a little mortar to put between the bricks, and I phoned him last in mid-July. In the background was the sound of children romping.

"It's raining like hell here," he said. "But I'm having fun with my two grandsons."

I asked him what was going on up there in his old Local 299. There had been some violence. In late June a man named Ralph Proctor, a Hoffa loyalist, had been beaten severely outside a Detroit bar. On July 10 a car owned by Richard Fitzsimmons, son of the man who deposed him as Teamster general president, was blown up outside the same bar.

"It's some nut," he said. "A guy trying to start trouble. But everybody in the local knows who he is."

That was the last time I talked to Jimmy Hoffa.

In mid-morning of Wednesday, July 30, Jimmy told his wife, Jo, that he was going to a meeting at 2 P.M. with "Tony Jack and a couple of other guys."

"Tony Jack," also known as "Tony J." and "T. J.," is Anthony Giacalone, reputed Detroit Mafia leader who was under indictment on income-tax-evasion and mail-fraud charges. Hoffa had been called before a grand jury to testify in the Giacalone case and—something he never did in his own defense—he had taken the Fifth to keep from discussing someone else's activities.

Driving through Pontiac, en route to the meeting, Hoffa stopped off at the Airport Service Lines, a limousine service, to see owner Louis Linteau, an old friend. Linteau was out to lunch and Hoffa talked to several employees, explaining that he had dropped in on his way to a meeting. He mentioned several names.

Leaving the limousine company's office, Hoffa drove to the Machus Red Fox restaurant, fifteen miles north of downtown Detroit, and parked his car in the north shopping center parking lot adjoining the restaurant.

At 2:30 P.M., Hoffa called his wife. "Giacalone didn't show up," he said. "Did he call? Where the hell is he?"

Josephine said that no one had called and Jimmy told her he would be home by 4 P.M. He also called Linteau and said the meeting didn't come off.

Four o'clock came and went but Hoffa did not arrive home. Ed Lawrenson telephoned from Washington at five o'clock and Josephine advised him that "Jimmy must have gotten tied up someplace." Lawrenson called back at 7:15 P.M. and Josephine said she had tired of waiting for dinner and yet was getting so worried she hadn't been able to eat.

"It was just not like him," Lawrenson explained. "He kept in constant touch with Jo. We traveled together more than two years on NAJ business and no matter where we went, as soon as we arrived he'd go to a phone and call her. It was a way of life; a religion with him.

"Jimmy was really soft about his family," Lawrenson added. "And he was considerate with his friends. When my wife Lillian had to have an operation in Washington he wanted to bring in a surgeon from Detroit to make sure everything went right. So you can understand that he was the kind of man who put his family ahead of everything else. Being gone without a word just wasn't like him."

Josephine Hoffa waited alone until 10 P.M. Then, completely distraught, she phoned Joe Bane, a Teamster official in Detroit and a longtime friend. Bane went to the Hoffa home and they then called young Jim, who was vacationing at isolated Traverse City, Michigan, and also Hoffa's daughter, Mrs. Barbara Crancer, in St. Louis.

The children arrived early the next morning at about the same time that Hoffa's car was discovered in the shopping center parking lot. The car was unlocked and there was some dirt on the front seat, but no signs of a struggle. Which has to say something, because no stranger could have taken Jimmy Hoffa without a titanic struggle.

On the calendar in Hoffa's room, under the date of July 30, was this memo in Hoffa's handwriting: "T. J.—2 P.M.— Red Fox."

Hoping desperately that Jimmy would appear, the family held off until six o'clock the next evening, July 31, before reporting him missing because they didn't want to create unnecessary publicity. Then Jimmy Hoffa became a number again: Missing Person Number 75-3425.

Late that night, Chuck O'Brien appeared at Lake Orion.

Right here let's clear up one mystery.

O'Brien was *not* a son of any kind to the Hoffas. He was *not* an adopted son *nor* a foster son and he had never lived in the Hoffa home.

When Jimmy said he had "practically raised him" he meant that after O'Brien's father died he had helped send O'Brien to a military school in Kansas City because of the long-standing friendship between the two families. When Jimmy said "he was more of a son of mine than a protégé," he was alluding to his fondness for and belief in the loyalty of a young man he had taken under his wing and given a union job when O'Brien was nineteen.

The "foster son" image was projected when O'Brien chauffeured Mrs. Hoffa to Lewisburg on family visiting days and, so that O'Brien could get in to see Jimmy too, they fabricated that he was Hoffa's "foster son."

But, as Hoffa said, "self-preservation" made O'Brien a turncoat and young Jimmy confirmed that "O'Brien pledged his allegiance to Fitzsimmons seven months earlier." As a result of this capitulation, O'Brien escaped being sent to Alaska and instead, as Hoffa had heard earlier, was being considered for "getting a plush assignment to Florida."

When O'Brien appeared at Lake Orion, young Jimmy became involved in an argument with him over his malfeasance and charged him with "knowing something" about Hoffa's disappearance. O'Brien stormed out.

"The only motive big enough had to come out of the union," young Jimmy said. "The powers that be had too much to lose if Dad won in 1976 and then found out from the books what they'd been doing with the pension-fund money."

On Friday, August 1, two days after the disappearance, the family asked three employees of the limousine service in Pontiac to submit to hypnosis in an effort to learn the names Hoffa had mentioned to them.

Dr. Bruce Danto, a psychiatrist hired by the Hoffa family, hypnotized Elmer Reeves and Merita Crane. Both Reeves and Miss Crane recalled Hoffa using the names Tony J. and Tony P. Linteau and Edgardo Solomon, the company bookkeeper, submitted to an injection of brevitol sodium, which induces a state of drowsiness and a lack of inhibitions and is similar to a preoperative anesthetic. Linteau said he knew Hoffa was to meet with Giacalone and that "Tony J." had called him several times previously to attempt to set up meetings with Hoffa. Solomon confirmed that Hoffa had mentioned "Tony J. and Tony P.," but none of them could remember the name of the third man.

"Tony P." is a nickname for Anthony Provenzano, the former Union City, New Jersey, Teamster official who was in Lewisburg on an extortion conviction during the time that Hoffa was there. Their friendship ended, as Hoffa said early in this book, because he wouldn't help Provenzano get back his Teamster pension.

Various sources hinted that the third man at the meeting was to have been Leonard Schultz, a Detroit labor consultant who had set up his sons as operators of the Southfield Athletic Club.

All three, Giacalone, Provenzano, and Schultz, denied the meeting was to be held and all had alibis. Giacalone asserted that he was at the Southfield A.C. all that afternoon.

The next day, on Saturday, August 2, Hoffa's children reported receiving extortion threats as well as a telephone call to their unlisted number threatening Linteau's life "if he don't keep his mouth shut." This permitted FBI intervention and two agents appeared on Sunday, August 3.

The family telephoned U.S. Attorney General Edward H. Levi and FBI Director Clarence M. Kelley to demand more concentrated action.

"You used two thousand agents to put my father in jail," said Hoffa's daughter, Barbara, "and you're only using two to find him."

The FBI, after years of aggressiveness toward Jimmy, finally took a gentle tack with the Hoffas. Subtly reproving, it told them that a dozen agents had been working on the case unofficially and that the FBI investigation now would become official.

The Hoffa children also demanded that Chuck O'Brien, who had vanished after his argument with young Jim, be given a lie-detector test. They said they were "sure O'Brien knows something."

O'Brien had been remarried secretly on June 16 and had gone to West Memphis, Arkansas, to be with his bride. On Monday, August 4, wearing a "Fitz in '76" button, he turned up in Boston to confer with Fitzsimmons. Hoffa's successor advised him to return to Detroit to be available to investigators. O'Brien went back on Wednesday, August 6, was questioned then and also later by the FBI, and his attorney asserted that O'Brien had "satisfied" the agents with his statements.

There was a brief flurry when blood was found in a car which O'Brien had borrowed the day Hoffa disappeared. He said it was blood from a salmon he had delivered to the home of a union official and tests proved it was fish blood. The family inferred that it was not a salmon but a red herring.

(Following national publicity that I was writing Hoffa's book, I received a telephone call at 2:30 P.M. on August 6. "Be careful what you put in Hoffa's book," said a muffled voice. "What?" I asked. "Just be careful what you put in Hoffa's book," the unidentified caller repeated. And hung up. Hoax? I don't know. To paraphrase Hoffa, I was careful to put every goddamned thing Jimmy ever told me into this book.)

The days passed into weeks and it revived memories of the Crater case of yesteryear. On August 6, 1930, New York Supreme Court Justice Joseph Force Crater left a restaurant in New York's Times Square, stepped into a taxicab, and never was seen again despite a search that went on for years from Hoboken to Hong Kong.

The city of New York offered a $5000 reward for Judge Crater. But the reward offers for Hoffa quickly jumped to a total of $325,000, including $200,000 by the family and $25,000 by his old Local 299.

In the interim there was a much-repeated rumor on the grapevine that Hoffa had been the victim of a million-dollar "hit" because underworld figures feared he would return to power and "blow the whistle" on vast pension-fund loans they had received. There were whispers that there had been a "leak" in Washington that the court was about to find in Hoffa's favor and cancel the conditions of his commutation. This was denied, but the mere hint of such a decision being readied could be regarded as dangerous to Hoffa's well-being.

It is interesting to note that:

It was belatedly announced on August 13 that the Southern Conference offices of the Teamsters were being moved from Dallas, Texas, to Hallandale, Florida, just north of Miami.

On August 14, Southern Conference Director Joseph Morgan told interviewers O'Brien had asked to be transferred to the Southern Conference *six months ago.*

That Frank Fitzsimmons owned a condominium in the Sky Lake Country Club complex in North Miami, within five miles of Hallandale.

That Anthony Giacalone has a plush $165,000 penthouse apartment in the Miami Beach Tower House, within ten miles of Hallandale.

That Anthony Provenzano has a $150,000 house in the posh Golden Isles section of Hallandale. This is the same "Tony Pro" who, when questioned shortly after Hoffa's disappearance, said, "Jimmy *was* . . . is . . . a friend."

Hoffa clearly was a Caesar who had more than one Brutus. And, as Mark Anthony mourned: "Whilst bloody treason flourish'd over us."

Remembering, you recall how Hoffa vowed, "I'll be back," and you wonder . . . and wonder . . .

Meanwhile the big rigs thundered over highways from coast to coast, many of them bearing a heartfelt bumper sticker:

"Where is Jimmy Hoffa?"

AFFIDAVIT

STATE OF MICHIGAN   )
                  :ss.
COUNTY OF WAYNE   )

James P. Hoffa, Jr., Josephine Hoffa and Barbara Crancer, being duly sworn, depose and say:

1. We have been aware of James R. Hoffa's contractual and close working relationship with Stein and Day, publishers, and Oscar Fraley, who agreed several months ago to help him to write the book about his life and his plans for the future. We are also aware that James R. Hoffa assigned all the proceeds stemming from that book to National Association for Justice.

2. We know that before James R. Hoffa's disappearance, he had many lengthy discussions with Mr. Fraley -- face to face and over the telephone -- for the purpose of preparing a manuscript of that book that recorded James R. Hoffa's thoughts, views and hopes in the words he chose to use.

3. The book that Stein and Day is to publish, with our authorization, contains the thoughts, views and hopes of James R. Hoffa, expressed in language we have often heard him use to convey those thoughts, views and hopes.

James P. Hoffa
James P. Hoffa, Jr.

Josephine Hoffa
Josephine Hoffa

Barbara Crancer
Barbara Crancer

Sworn to before me this
29th day of August 1975.

Patricia M. Moran
Notary Public

PATRICIA M. MORAN
Notary Public, Wayne County, Michigan
My Commission Expires January 17, 1978

Stein and Day Paperbacks

★

TITLE	AUTHOR	PRICE
Add Years to Your Life and Life to Your Years	*Dr. Irene Gore*	$1.95
Alexander Pope	*Peter Quennell*	$2.95
America America	*Elia Kazan*	$1.95
Aspects of Wagner	*Bryan Magee*	$1.25
Being Busted	*Leslie Fiedler*	$1.95
Bessie	*Chris Albertson*	$2.95
Black and White	*Brigid Brophy*	$1.95
Blacks, Whites and Blues	*Anthony Russell*	$1.95
Bobby Fischer vs. the Rest of the World	*Brad Darrach*	$2.95
The Book of Longer Short Stories	*James Michie, ed.*	$4.95
Caruso	*Stanley Jackson*	$3.95
Chaliapin	*Maxim Gorky*	$3.95
Ché Guevara	*Daniel James*	$3.95
Childhood Illness	*Jack Shiller, M.D.*	$2.45
The Complete Bolivian Diaries of Ché Guevara	*Daniel James, ed.*	$2.95
Cross the Border—Close the Gap	*Leslie Fiedler*	$2.95
Dando Shaft	*Don Calhoun*	$1.50
Deafness	*David Wright*	$1.95
Dictionary of Battles	*Thomas Harbottle*	$4.95
The Difficult Child	*A. J. Montanari & Arthur Henley*	$1.95
Dossier	*Aryeh Neier*	$2.45
Eating in Eight Languages	*Wilma George*	$1.95
An End to Innocence	*Leslie Fiedler*	$2.95
Erasmus	*George Faludy*	$2.95

TITLE	AUTHOR	PRICE
The Fabulous Life of Diego Rivera	Bertram D. Wolfe	$3.95
The Femininity Game	Thomas Boslooper & Marcia Hayes	$1.95
Fifty Works of English & American Literature We Could Do Without	Brigid Brophy, Michael Levey, & Charles Osborne	$1.95
Food in History	Reay Tannahill	$4.95
Forbidden Universe	Leo Talamonti	$2.45
Friendship	Myron Brenton	$2.45
From Satchmo To Miles	Leonard Feather	$2.95
From Time to Time	Hannah Tillich	$1.95
G. K. Chesterton	Dudley Barker	$3.95
Gandhi	Geoffrey Ashe	$3.95
The Gay Mystique	Peter Thomas Fisher	$1.95
Good Memory—Good Student!	Harry Lorayne	$1.95
Good Memory—Successful Student!	Harry Lorayne	$1.95
A Handbook of Underwater Exploration	Bill St. John Wilkes	$2.45
Help Without Psychoanalysis	Dr. Herbert Fensterheim	$2.45
The History of World Cinema	David Robinson	$4.95
The Hitchhiker's Guide to Europe	Ken Welsh	$1.95
The House of Krupp	Peter Batty	$2.95
How It All Began	Miles Wolff, Jr.	$1.95
How To Avoid Social Diseases	Leslie Nicholas, M.D.	$2.25
How To Raise Children At Home In Your Spare Time	Marvin Gersh	$1.95
How To Teach Your Baby to Swim	Claire Timmermans	$2.95
How Will You Feel Tomorrow?	Samuel Silverman, M.D.	$2.95
An Ideology in Power	Bertram D. Wolfe	$2.95
Israel: Land of Promise	Arthur Tcholakian	$4.95
It Usually Begins With Ayn Rand	Jerome Tuccille	$2.95
Jean Genet	Philip Thody	$2.45

TITLE	AUTHOR	PRICE
Joan of Arc	*Régine Pernoud*	$2.95
Khrushchev	*Mark Frankland*	$2.95
The Kids' Own XYZ of Love and Sex	*Siv Widerberg*	$2.25
Kings and Queens of England	*Eric R. Delderfield*	$2.25
Landowska on Music	*Denise Restout & Robert Hawkins, eds.*	$4.95
The Life and Death of Mozart	*Michael Levey*	$3.95
The Life and Times of Muhammad	*Sir John Glubb*	$2.95
Living is Loving	*Inge & Sten Hegeler*	$1.95
Love and Death in the American Novel	*Leslie Fiedler*	$4.95
Ma Rainey and the Classic Blues Singers	*Derrick Stewart Baxter*	$1.95
Major International Treaties	*J. A. S. Grenville*	$8.95
The Man of Principle	*Dudley Barker*	$2.45
Mastering Herbalism	*Paul Huson*	$4.95
Match Your Skills Against the Masters	*Jeremy Flint & Freddie North*	$1.95
Mayday 747	*Reynolds Locke*	$2.45
The Mayflower	*Kate Caffrey*	$3.95
The Modern Family Guide to Dental Health	*A. Norman Cranin, DDS*	$2.95
Mother Is	*Siv Cedering Fox*	$2.95
The Mystic Healers	*Paris Flammonde*	$2.45
The New Anatomy of Britain	*Anthony Sampson*	$4.95
No! In Thunder	*Leslie Fiedler*	$2.95
Non-Human Thought	*Jacques Graven*	$1.95
Nude Croquet	*Leslie Fiedler*	$1.95
The Obscenity Report	*Anonymous*	$2.95
Olivier	*Logan Gourlay*	$2.95
Petrovka 38	*Julian Semyonov*	$1.95

TITLE	AUTHOR	PRICE
The Politics of Rape	*Diana E. H. Russell*	$3.95
The Powers of Hypnosis	*Jean Dauven*	$2.45
Recording The Blues	*R. M. W. Dixon &* *John Godrich*	$1.95
The Return of the Vanishing American	*Leslie Fiedler*	$2.95
The Sacred Books of the Jews	*Harry Gersh*	$2.95
Samuel Taylor Coleridge	*Molly Lefebure*	$5.95
Sappho Was A Right-On Woman	*Sidney Abbott &* *Barbara Love*	$1.95
Savannah Syncopators	*Paul Oliver*	$2.50
The Scientific Basis Of Astrology	*Michel Gauquelin*	$2.45
Sense Of Direction	*John Fernald*	$1.95
Seven Days Of Freedom	*Noel Barber*	$2.95
Sex and the Confessional	*Norberto Valentini &* *Clara Dimeglio*	$1.95
A Short History Of the Arab Peoples	*Sir John Glubb*	$2.95
The Six Day War	*David Kimche &* *Dan Bawley*	$2.95
Solzhenitsyn	*David Burg &* *George Feifer*	$3.95
Stalin	*Leon Trotsky*	$3.95
Starting Out	*Lili Krakowski*	$2.95
The Stein and Day Handbook of Magic	*Marvin Kaye*	$2.95
Stories Cops Only Tell Each Other	*Gene Radano*	$1.95
The Stranger In Shakespeare	*Leslie Fiedler*	$2.95
Talking To Animals	*Barbara Woodhouse*	$1.95
This Is Your Captain Speaking	*Thomas Ashwood*	$1.95
Three Billion Years of Life	*Andre de Cayeux*	$2.45
Total Self-Knowledge	*Ernest Dichter*	$4.95
To The Gentiles	*Leslie Fiedler*	$2.95

TITLE	AUTHOR	PRICE
The Truth About Dracula	Gabriel Ronay	$1.95
Underdog	Mordecai Siegal & Matthew Margolis	$2.45
Unfinished Business	Leslie Fiedler	$2.95
The Vocabulary of Science	Lancelot Hogben	$1.95
Waiting For The End	Leslie Fiedler	$2.95
The Warburgs	David Farrer	$2.45
When I Put Out To Sea	Nicolette Milnes Walker	$2.45
The Who	Jeff Stein & Chris Johnston	$3.95
The Wit and Wisdom of Harry S. Truman	George S. Caldwell	$1.50
A Woman's Guide To The Care and Feeding of an Automobile	Carmel B. Reingold	$1.95
The Worlds of Truman Capote	William L. Nance	$2.95

Buy them at your local bookstore or use this handy coupon for ordering.

Stein and Day / Publishers
Scarborough House, Briarcliff Manor, N.Y. 10510

Please send me the books listed below. I am enclosing $_____ (please add 25¢ for one book and 9¢ for each additional book ordered to cover postage and handling. Send check or money order—no cash or C.O.D.'s please).

Name_____

Address_____

City_____ State / Zip_____

TITLES_____

_____